The Strategic Defense Initiative

Guides to Contemporary Issues

Richard Dean Burns, Editor

This series is devoted to exploring contemporary social, political, economic, diplomatic and military issues. Each guide begins with an extended narrative which introduces opinions and interpretations regarding the issue under discussion, and concludes with a comprehensive bibliographical survey of the essential writings on the topic, including recent articles, books, and documents. The guides, consequently, are designed to provide reference librarians, academic researchers, students, and informed citizens with easy access to information concerning controversial issues.

This series has been developed, in part, in cooperation with the Center for the Study of Armament and Disarmament, California State University, Los Angeles, California.

#1 THE MX CONTROVERSY
Robert A. Hoover

#2 THE MILITARY IN THE DEVELOPMENT PROCESS
Nicole Ball

#3 THE PERSIAN GULF & UNITED STATES POLICY
Bruce R. Kuniholm

#4 CENTRAL AMERICA & UNITED STATES POLICIES, 1820s-1980s
Thomas M. Leonard

#5 THE PALESTINIAN PROBLEM & UNITED STATES POLICY
Bruce R. Kuniholm & Michael Rubner

#6 FAMINE: A HERITAGE OF HUNGER
Arline T. Golkin

#7 THE STRATEGIC DEFENSE INITIATIVE
Douglas C. Waller, James T. Bruce, & Douglas M. Cook

THE STRATEGIC DEFENSE INITIATIVE

Progress and Challenges

A Guide to Issues and References

Douglas C. Waller
James T. Bruce
Douglas M. Cook

REGINA BOOKS
Claremont, California

Library of Congress Cataloging in Publication Data

Waller, Douglas C.
   The Strategic Defense Initiative, progress and challenges.

   (Guides to contemporary issues : # 7)
   Biography: p.
   Includes index.
   1. Strategic Defense Initiative. **I.** Bruce, James, 1947-   . **II.** Cook,
Douglas M., 1949-   . **III.** Title. **IV.** Series.
   UG743.W355 1987   358'.1754   87-14820

ISBN 0-941690-24-5
ISBN 0-941690-25-3 (pbk.)

Regina Books
P.O. Box 280
Claremont, Ca. 91711

Manufactured in the United States of America.

Contents

List of Illustrations

Preface

This book is based primarily on a congressional staff report (and a subsequent update) which Senators William Proxmire, J. Bennett Johnston, and Lawton Chiles directed us to undertake at the beginning of 1986. During the six months preceding 1986, senior officials in the White House, Department of Defense, and the Strategic Defense Initiative Organization (SDIO) had been quoted in the press as saying that President Reagan's Strategic Defense Initiative (SDI) had made tremendous progress since the program's inception. Adjectives such as "incredible" and "amazing" had been used—and still are being used—by these officials to describe research breakthroughs SDI has achieved. The Strategic Defense Initiative had been designated a research program to determine the feasibility of a comprehensive ballistic missile defense system to shield both military and civilian targets from Soviet nuclear weapons. These so-called breakthroughs have been and are being cited as evidence that SDI is feasible and that the unprecedented level of funding requested for this research program is justified.

The senators, who serve on the Defense Appropriations Subcommittee, requested this study to learn more about the actual progress made in SDI research and the problems and challenges that lie ahead for the program. This book is not meant to be an comprehensive assessment of SDI. Rather, it attempts to highlight what appear to be key issues related to SDI's progress and problems, which policy analysts and policy makers may wish to consider.

We began our research in 1986 by visiting and receiving extensive briefings at the following facilities conducting SDI research:

- The U.S. Army Strategic Defense Command, Huntsville, Alabama. The Army, along with the Air Force, has been designated by the Strategic Defense Initiative Organization to execute the largest portion of the SDI budget. The Army's Strategic Defense Command conducts research into terminal defense for the SDI system (destroying Soviet warheads as they reenter the atmosphere and speed to the U.S.) and anti-tactical ballistic missiles suitable for a European defense.

- The U.S. Air Force Space Division, Los Angeles, California. One of five divisions of the Air Force Space Command, the Space Division manages that service's execution of SDI research, concentrating on boost-phase defense (destroying Soviet missiles shortly after they leave the launch pad while the booster rocket is still firing), post-boost phase defense (destroying the bus of warheads the missile dispenses), and midcourse defense (destroying warheads as they travel through space).

- The Sandia National Laboratory, Albuquerque, New Mexico. Sandia is conducting research into the Soviet offensive threat SDI would face, SDI systems, warhead discrimination technology, and space power.

- The Lawrence Livermore National Laboratory, Livermore, California. Livermore is conducting research in directed energy weapons such as X-ray lasers and free electron lasers, in threat analysis, and in supercomputers.

In addition to visiting major SDI facilities, we received briefings from the Strategic Defense Initiative Organization's director Lieutenant General James Abrahamson, SDIO's five program managers, its European strategic defense specialists, the General Accounting Office, the Defense Intelligence Agency, and other scientists and ballistic missile defense experts. *One unique feature of our study was that its information was compiled not from SDI's critics, but from more than 40 top scientists, engineers, managers, and experts deeply involved with and supportive of SDI research.*

This book is also drawn from an updated SDI staff report that was issued in March 1987. For that updated report, two of the authors revisited the Sandia and Livermore labs and the Air Force Space Division. Visits also were made to two defense contractors performing SDI work and to the Los Alamos National Laboratory in Los Alamos, New Mexico, which is conducting extensive research into various directed energy concepts. In all, more than sixty experts were interviewed during this second phase.

We are indebted to a number of people, many of whom cannot be named, for their assistance in the preparation and publication of this book. Most importantly, we owe a debt of gratitude to Senators Proxmire, Johnston, and Chiles for allowing us to undertake the initial study and for guiding its scope and direction. We also thank General Abrahamson, his staff, and the SDI scientists for the thorough briefings they gave us.

The book benefited from the advice and counsel of many defense and legislative aides in the Senate. In particular, we thank Ronald Tammen, Richard Brandon, and Michael Harvey for their advice and support in preparing this report. Dr. Sidney Drell, deputy director of the Stanford Linear Accelerator Center, also gave us invaluable technical advice as did John Pike, associate director for space policy at the Federation of American Scientists.

Finally, we would like to thank our wives, without whose advice, encouragement, and patience this book would not have been possible.

Douglas C. Waller
James T. Bruce
Douglas Cook

Washington, D.C.
1987

ABM & SDI Chronology

Late 1950s & early 1960s	U.S. Army seeks to produce Nike-Zeus anti-ballistic missile (ABM) system for nation-wide defense. Eisenhower and Kennedy administrations refuse, questioning its effectiveness.
1959	Defense Department begins the *Ballistic Missile Boost Intercept* (BAMBI) program to study intercepts of ICBMs in the boost phase with interceptors based on satellites.
1963	Defense budget authorizes research on Nike-X ABM system (later "Sprint") to intercept ICBMs after re-entering the atmosphere. BAMBI is cancelled.
1965	Phyllis Schlafly and Chester Ward in *Strike from Space* argue that the U.S. should develop ABM space defenses and offensive arms to "win the military space race."
1965	U.S. Army initiates "Spartan" ABM system to intercept ICBMs outside the atmosphere.
1966	Soviets had begun deploying an ABM system. President Johnson's FY 1968 budget calls for Nike-X (Sprint & Spartan) deployment in January 1967, to protect U.S. cities but postpones deployment decision pending ABM limitation talks.

September 18, 1967   Defense Secretary Robert McNamara opposes an ABM system to protect cities because Soviets would overcome it and a costly escalation of the arms race would result. He proposes a *partial* ABM system ("Sentinel") as insurance against Chinese or accidental Soviet attacks.

August 1968   Soviet invasion of Czechoslovakia ends ABM negotiations.

January 1969   President Nixon's Defense Secretary Melvin Laird suspends Sentinel deployment and reviews the ABM program.

March 1969   Nixon proposes the "Safeguard" ABM system to defend Minuteman ICBMs. He rejects ABM defense of U.S. cities as ineffective and threatening to the Soviet deterrent.

1969   Congressional debate begins over ABM following extensive public protest. Safeguard system passes on a 50-50 tie vote in Senate.

U.S. develops Multiple Independently-targeted Reentry Vehicles (MIRVs) to counter anticipated Soviet ABM system.

May 1972   SALT I agreement reached at Helsinki includes the treaty on "The Limitation of Anti-Ballistic Missile Systems," which sharply restricts the development, testing, and deployment of ABM systems.

1974   U.S. and U.S.S.R. limit ABM deployment of 100 interceptors to only one of the two areas provided for in the Treaty.

1976   For cost reasons and questionable effectiveness, the U.S. deactivates its only ABM system at Grand Forks, North Dakota.

1981-1982   Reagan's Defense and State departments review "High Frontier" proposals for ballistic missile defense and reject them.

1983

Defense budget includes approximately $1 billion for ABM research and deployment.

March 23, 1983

President Reagan proposes in his "Star Wars" speech a national research program to render nuclear weapons "impotent and obsolete."

March 29, 1983

Reagan says neither a crash program nor additional funding above the current $1 billion is necessary for SDI.

October 1983

Future Security Strategy Study Team, chaired by Fred S. Hoffman, assesses the role of defensive systems in future U.S. national security strategy.

January 1984

Defense Department establishes the Strategic Defense Initiative Organization (SDIO) to determine the feasibility of an effective ballistic missile defense.

March 1984

The "Defensive Technologies Study Team" report (Fletcher Report) becomes the blueprint for the SDI research program. The report recommends a *crash program* on SDI but concedes a less costly program could achieve necessary technology with some delay.

October 21, 1984

Reagan says he would "give" SDI technology to the Soviets.

March 4, 1985

In a press conference Reagan claims he conceived the idea of SDI, particularly the boost-phase defense. However, Project BAMBI (1961) and High Frontier (1981) predated his idea.

May 1985

Over half the membership of the National Academy of Science and the living American Nobel Laureates petition the U.S. and U.S.S.R. to negotiate a treaty banning the testing and deployment of weapons in space.

October 6, 1985	Robert McFarlane, National Security Adviser, announces that the ABM treaty permits testing and development of ABM systems based on "other physical principles."
October 25, 1985	Reagan offers to share SDI technology with the Soviets.
October 31, 1985	Reagan states the U.S. will not deploy SDI "until we do away with our nuclear missiles," but the U.S. will make SDI available to the Soviet Union.
November 6, 1985	Reagan says he has been misunderstood. If the Soviets do not agree to eliminate nuclear weapons, the U.S. would deploy SDI, even though the Soviets might believe the U.S. was seeking a first-strike capability.
November 11, 1985	Director of the SDI Organization, Lt. Gen. James Abrahamson, says there are "only a few diehards left" critical of SDI.
December 1985	A report by the SDI Panel on Computing in Support of Battle Management (Eastport Study Group) concludes that computer software and hardware for SDI are possible but will be extremely complex.
January 30, 1986	French government releases a study (Delpech Report) which concludes that a space defense system cannot be operational before 2010 and that a medium power such as France "could probably acquire the means to partially neutralize a space defense system, or at least to degrade its performance sufficiently to ensure the penetration of its own ballistic missiles."
March 1986	A poll of the American Physical Society shows 67% of the respondents believe it is "improbable" or "very unlikely" that SDI could protect American cities from a Soviet attack.
March 5, 1986	General Abrahamson says SDI is technically feasible but cost effectiveness remains to be determined.

April 10, 1986

Former Defense Secretary Harold Brown estimates the costs of SDI deployment: "I think a trillion dollars may be an underestimate."

May 1986

A petition signed by 6,500 scientists and engineers, including 15 Nobel Laureates and a majority of the faculty from the top 20 university physics departments, opposes SDI.

May 22, 1986

Forty-six senators sign a letter questioning need for increasing SDI's budget more than 3% for FY 1987. The president had requested a 78% increase.

June 2, 1986

Two additional senators sign the letter questioning SDI's accelerated funding.

June 19, 1986

Over 1,600 scientists and engineers from private and government laboratories question the pace of SDI research and the lack of technical and policy scrutiny, and ask that SDI be limited to "a scale appropriate to exploratory research."

President Reagan says the SDI shield "could protect us from nuclear missiles just as a roof protects a family from rain."

June 23, 1986

Time quotes Richard Perle, an assistant secretary of defense, as saying SDI would not defend cities but rather U.S. capacity to retaliate.

July 8, 1986

Senate Armed Services Committee rejects Reagan's vision of an astrodome defense shield for the U.S. and calls for a realistic reorientation of the SDI program.

August 4-5, 1986

Senate amendment to reduce funds for SDI to $3.2 billion rather than the $3.9 billion approved by the Armed Services Committee fails by a 1-vote margin.

August 12, 1986

House approves a funding level of $3.1 billion for SDI in FY 1987.

October 1, 1986

SDI's strongest supporters urge Reagan to begin early deployment of SDI.

October 11-12, 1986

Reagan and Soviet General Secretary Mikhail Gorbachev meet in Reykjavik, Iceland. The summit talks collapse when Reagan refuses to accept limitations on SDI in exchange for deep reductions in Soviet offensive nuclear forces.

October 15, 1986

Congress approves $3.5 billion for SDI, cutting nearly $2 billion from the president's original request.

October 30, 1986

A poll of the National Academy of Sciences shows 78% of respondents believe prospects in the next 25 years are poor or extremely poor that SDI can be made survivable and cost-effective. Only 3.6% believe the prospects are extremely good or good that these criteria will be met.

January 14, 1987

Attorney General Edwin Meese III says the administration should deploy the first stage of SDI "so it will be in place and not tampered with by future administrations.

January 22, 1987

Secretary of Defense Caspar Weinberger says "Today, we may be nearing the day when decisions about deployment of the first phase [of SDI] can be made."

March 11-13, 1987

Sam Nunn, chairman of the Senate Armed Services Committee challenges the administration's contention that the ABM Treaty permits testing and developing of SDI systems.

April 1987

American Physical Society releases its study, "Science and Technology of Directed Energy Weapons," which concludes that a decade or more of intensive research is necessary to determine the effectiveness and survivability of directed energy weapons.

Introduction

On March 23, 1983, as the nuclear freeze movement gained increasing support across the country and the Pentagon budget came under attack in Congress, President Ronald Reagan took to the airwaves to plead for higher spending for national defense. In a televised address to the nation, the president again insisted that U.S. national security was imperiled by ever-increasing Soviet military might. Wedged into this speech was a short passage which few of Reagan's advisers had been made aware of in advance.

That passage (see Appendix A) called for a comprehensive scientific research effort to render nuclear weapons "impotent and obsolete"—in other words, to determine if we could erect a shield or defense system that would destroy Soviet missiles and warheads before they reached U.S. soil. Raising questions that had not been debated nationally since the 1960s, Reagan asked:

> What if free people could live secure in the knowledge that their security did not rest upon the threat of instant retaliation to deter a Soviet attack, that we could intercept and destroy strategic ballistic missiles before they reached our own soil or that of our allies?

For three decades, the U.S. has relied ultimately on massive nuclear retaliation to deter a Soviet nuclear attack on this country. The standoff has become known as Mutual Assured Destruction (MAD)—a doctrine which holds that a retaliatory response from the U.S. (even after suffering a Soviet first strike) would be so devastating that it would deter a Soviet leader from ever initiating a nuclear strike. U.S. nuclear deterrence also has been extended to our North Atlantic Treaty Organization allies who face a sizeable Warsaw Pact conventional force.

Over the years, nuclear weapons and strategies have been refined by both superpowers. Both can now deliver nuclear arms with pinpoint accuracy, thus theoretically threatening each side's missile silos and hardened military targets. U.S. and Soviet leaders also have a variety of response options, such as limited nuclear strikes ("flexible response") that destroy selected military targets. Most military strategists concede, however, that any type of nuclear conflict between the United States and the Soviet Union would likely escalate in short order to all-out nuclear war and destroy civilization as we know it. This realization has kept an uneasy peace the past three decades and "for Western security," as former Defense Secretary James Schlesinger recently wrote, "the nuclear deterrent continues to represent the ultimate reality."

Past American presidents, however, have been uncomfortable with this reality—that U.S. national security rests upon the threat of nuclear annihilation—yet they largely resigned themselves to this situation. Reagan, however, turned MAD on its head and proposed that the superpowers would be more secure if they defended against the other's nuclear threat. Both nations would move from mutual assured destruction to mutual assured survival. It was not a new idea.

From the late 1960s to the early 1970s the U.S., which had developed nuclear-armed missile interceptors for its air defense fleet, pursued the idea of ballistic missile defenses. The Soviet Union had also developed an interceptor missile system, known as Galosh.

By 1972, however, evidence indicated that an effective comprehensive ballistic missile defense (BMD) system could not be deployed: it would be too expensive, and it would likely instigate a dangerous offensive-defensive arms race. The Anti-Ballistic Missile (ABM) Treaty signed that year sharply limited

ABM development, testing, and deployment for both sides (see Appendix B).

Since entering into the ABM Treaty, the U. S. has continued research into ballistic missile defense technology, concentrating on low-altitude, nuclear-armed interceptors and non-nuclear exoatmospheric interceptors that might be deployed in a few years in response to a Soviet "breakout" or sudden termination of the ABM Treaty. Some work was conducted in exotic technologies, such as lasers, which might have long-term applications; however, this research was scattered throughout a number of agencies and military services and lacked overall focus or direction. All told, less than one billion dollars was spent annually on research into ballistic missile defense (BMD) and related technologies in the years immediately preceding Reagan's "Star Wars" speech.

Although the U.S. saw no compelling economic or military justification for an ABM deployment as provided for in the treaty, the Soviet Union deployed Galosh interceptors around Moscow, which are currently being modernized. The Moscow ABM system, which is based on technology the U.S. had developed at least 10 years ago, would be largely ineffective against a concentrated U.S. attack. Nevertheless, the Moscow ABM system does provide operational training for Soviet troops, which is not available for their U.S. counterparts.

The Soviets also have in place an extensive air defense network for use against aircraft and air-breathing cruise missiles, which some have speculated could easily be converted to ABM defense. This capability, combined with an expansion of the current ABM system around Moscow, "suggests that the U.S.S.R. may be preparing an ABM defense of its national territory," according to the Department of Defense's 1985 edition of *Soviet Military Power*.

Other intelligence estimates, such as one provided by the Central Intelligence Agency (CIA) in unclassified testimony before the Senate's Defense Appropriations Subcommittee on June 26, 1985, do not come to the same conclusion. They pointed to evidence suggesting that Soviet air defenses will likely not be associated with strategic defense and that the Moscow ABM system would likely not be expanded in the near future.

This latter assessment is plausible because Soviet ABM interceptor rockets are nuclear tipped, making them more suitable for defending hardened military targets than cities, which could be damaged by the interceptor's nuclear explosion. Military targets also would likely have priority in an expanded Soviet missile defense. "It will be a long time before they [the Soviets] will do civilian defense," a Defense Intelligence Agency briefer told us. "It's not in their cards."

The Soviets also have conducted extensive research into laser and particle beam technology; however, U.S. intelligence analysts are vague and not unanimous in their assessment of how much progress the Soviets have actually made in this research and in advancing its military utility.

Before the president's March 1983 speech, there was general agreement within the defense community and in the Congress that the U.S. needed to conduct research in ballistic missile defenses as a hedge against a Soviet breakout or technological surprise and to explore emerging new technologies. To this day, among critics and supporters of SDI, there is general agreement that the U.S. should continue vigorous research into ballistic missile defenses.

It also had been widely acknowledged that funding for BMD research needed to be increased from its 1970s level, which is what the administration had planned to do, before the President's "Star Wars" speech. For example, the administration had hoped to increase the Department of Defense's (DoD) portion of strategic defense from $991 million in FY 1984 to $1.5 billion and $1.8 billion in FY 1985 and FY 1986 respectively, for a total of about $12.1 billion over five years (see Figure 1). Department of Energy spending for SDI-related activities was to total $1.8 billion for that same period.

Although there has been widespread support for a vigorous research and development (R&D) program in ballistic missile defenses to protect intercontinental ballistic missile (ICBM) silos (as a hedge against Soviet "breakout" of the ABM Treaty), there were few proponents within the military and scientific communities of a comprehensive defensive scheme to protect both military and civilian targets from Soviet attack. Thus, on March

23, 1983, President Reagan surprised most of the scientific and defense community by announcing that he was launching a national research effort with the "ultimate goal of eliminating the threat posed by strategic nuclear missiles."

Figure 1
Planned Funding for Strategic Defense
Before the President's March 23, 1983 Speech
($ million)

	FY84	FY85	FY86	FY87	FY88	FY89
Army	508	992	1,105	1,325	1,493	1,519
Navy	12	15	8	8	11	2
Air Force	146	195	348	440	722	929
DARPA	302	305	316	382	447	501
DNA	17	20	25	26	26	31
Total DoD	991	1,527	1,802	2,181	2,699	2,982
DoE		210	295	365	439	505
Total		1,737	2,097	2,546	3,138	3,487

Source: Strategic Defense Initiative Organization

Following the president's speech, the administration formed the Defensive Technology Study Team (the Fletcher Panel) made-up of ballistic missile defense experts. The Fletcher Panel, set up to define a long-term research and development program designed to eliminate the threat posed by ballistic missiles, produced a general blueprint for Star Wars research. Defense Secretary Caspar Weinberger used it to establish formally the Strategic Defense Initiative in January 1984. The Fletcher Panel's recommendations also became the basis for SDI's budget proposals for fiscal years 1985, 1986, and 1987. Another panel was formed after the president's speech, the Future Security Strategy Study Team, chaired by Fred S. Hoffman, which assessed the national security role of future strategic defenses.

Since its inception, SDI has touched off an intense debate in the defense and arms control community over the role of ballistic missile defense in U.S. national security. The debate also has caused deep divisions within the scientific community over the feasibility of such defenses.

Star Wars proponents maintain that "killing missiles" under mutual assured survival is a more humane and moral national security policy than "killing people" under mutual assured destruction. They argue that dramatic advances during the past decade in laser, sensor, rocket, and computer technology make a comprehensive ballistic missile defense shield possible, perhaps before the end of the century. They also insist that SDI is not really an initiative, but an effort to match an already robust Soviet BMD research program. Many Star Wars advocates believe that arms control has weakened U.S. national security and failed to contain Soviet nuclear force expansion over the past thirty years; ballistic missile defenses, on the other hand, would accomplish what arms control has failed to do—eliminate the danger of nuclear war by rendering offensive nuclear forces ineffective.

In considering whether a comprehensive missile defense system is feasible—that is, whether a shield similar to an impenetrable astrodome could be erected over the United States— three points should be kept in mind.

First, the charter of the Strategic Defense Initiative Organization (SDIO) directs it to conduct research to determine the *feasibility of an effective ballistic missile defense.* Neither the SDIO charter nor the SDI research effort itself is aimed at making nuclear weapons obsolete. It could not do so even if that were its aim. To make nuclear weapons obsolete would necessitate an absolutely perfect defense against all Soviet aircraft and cruise missiles, as well as against all ballistic missiles including those launched close to America's shores by submarines. As the Hoffman study noted, "pursuit of the President's goal...will raise questions about our readiness to defend against other threats, notably that of air attack by possible advanced bombers and cruise missiles. An appropriate response to such questions will require an early and comprehensive review of air defense technologies, leading to the development of useful systems concepts." An appropriate response also would require countering other means of delivering nuclear weapons—smuggled in by trawler, carried surreptitiously across the border in a suitcase, etc.

Second, during our briefings by the director of the SDI Organization, Lieutenant General James Abrahamson, and his program managers, there was never any discussion of an impenetrable defense shield against ballistic missiles that would protect all Americans from nuclear war. Rather, the SDI program is aimed ultimately at creating, for population defense, a system of successive layers of ballistic missile defenses, effective enough as a whole to deter the Soviets from attacking in the first place. General Abrahamson made it quite clear that the objective of SDI is *deterrence*.

President Reagan also has emphasized this point. In a 1985 interview, he said: "I've never asked for 100 percent. That would be a fine goal, but you can have a most effective defensive weapon even if it isn't 100 percent, because what you would have is the knowledge that—or that the other fellow would have the knowledge that if they launched a first strike, that it might be such that not enough of their missiles could get through, and in return we could launch the retaliatory strike.... If SDI is, say, 80 percent effective, then it will make any Soviet attack folly. Even partial success in SDI would strengthen deterrence and keep the peace."

In other words, with or without SDI, Soviet fear of our offensive force will remain the bulwark of U.S. deterrence.

Third, the feasibility of a comprehensive ballistic missile defense must be considered against very specific and demanding criteria, applied not just to individual weapon technologies, but to the system as a whole. These criteria include the system's affordability, its survivability, and the nature of future Soviet threats. There is no doubt that the U.S. eventually could build some type of ABM system that would be of limited effectiveness against a Soviet nuclear attack. However, a comprehensive strategic defense is an entirely different question and the criteria against which it will be measured are considerably more challenging. They are crucial nonetheless. A comprehensive ballistic missile defense will not prove to be feasible if they are not met.

In the fall of 1985, however, senior administration and DoD officials began making optimistic assessments of SDI's feasibility, asserting that substantial progress in the program had allayed many of the concerns that had been raised by outside critics. These comments came shortly after the summit in Geneva between President Reagan and Soviet General Secretary Mikhail Gorbachev.

General Abrahamson, for example, was quoted in the *New York Times* (Nov. 11, 1985) as saying that SDI's critics now consisted of

> only a few diehards left, sincere diehards, but only a very few, who still say this doesn't make sense, or who ask why we should do this to begin with.... The question is no longer can we do such a thing, but when, how fast and at what cost.

Using phrases such as "incredible" and "genuine breakthroughs," General Abrahamson claimed, according to press reports, that recent experiments have exceeded the program's most ambitious expectations.

In the same vein, Secretary of Defense Caspar Weinberger has been quoted as saying SDI is "making much greater progress than we anticipated. The barriers we saw to progress are crumbling." Then-White House science adviser George A. Keyworth II, meanwhile, told the *Washington Times*, "There have been monumental breakthroughs that have made us far more confident 2 1/2 years later than we projected even in the optimistic tone that was evident in the original [SDI] speech." Keyworth went on to claim that the U.S. would be able to demonstrate the technical feasibility of a laser-based ABM system "if not in Ronald Reagan's tenure, then very shortly thereafter....Whoever is president in the early 1990s will have...sufficient information to think seriously about deployment."

Keyworth's statement suggested even more progress in SDI research than claimed by General Abrahamson and Secretary Weinberger. In the past, SDIO stated its goal was to be able to provide adequate information to make a development decision by the early 1990s—that is, a decision on SDI's feasibility and on whether to begin development of the weapons. A deployment decision would come later. Keyworth, however, seemed to indicate SDI research had progressed so rapidly, that the development decision might be made before the end of President Reagan's term and the deployment decision might be made in the early 1990s.

In addition to numerous public statements, SDI officials released results of recent experiments (along with photos and film), to demonstrate that substantial progress had been made. These releases, for example, included videotapes of a chemical laser shooting through the skin of a stationary mock-up of a Titan booster and what was reported to be a railgun destroying a missile booster under simulated flight conditions.

As previously noted, our study provides some perspective on the progress achieved to date in the Strategic Defense Initiative compared to the challenges that lie ahead for the program. Specifically, the study suggests seven findings:

(1) While some significant progress has been achieved in each of the five major programs of the Strategic Defense Initiative, none of it could be described as "amazing." Interviews with key SDI scientists involved in the research revealed that there have been *no major breakthroughs* which make a mid- to late-1990s deployment of comprehensive missile defenses more feasible than it was four years ago.

(2) In fact, the "schedule-driven" nature of the current research program, which requires that a development decision be made by the early 1990s, has aroused significant concern among scientists at the national weapons laboratories. The concern is twofold. First, promising long-term research will be compromised to reach an arbitrary schedule. Second, in an effort to maintain public support for high funding levels and an early development decision, SDI experiments will degenerate, in the words of a senior scientist at the Livermore National Laboratory, into "a series of sleazy stunts."

(3) Since its inception, the SDI has undergone radical shifts in its priorities. The latest is a reorientation of its program to vigorously pursue an early deployment of ballistic missile defenses, possibly by 1994-1995.

(4) Much of the progress that has been achieved has resulted in a greater understanding of program difficulties, which are much more severe than previously considered. Briefly, they are:

— The high-leverage, boost-phase defense that would intercept Soviet missiles shortly after they leave their silos faces considerable difficulties with survivability, which are greater than the obvious technical difficulties of developing operational weapons systems. A senior SDI researcher at the Sandia National Laboratory suggested that the technical problem of survivability was so intractable that the solution might well be a joint U.S.- Soviet space station to coordinate space-based defense efforts.

— If the boost-phase defense proves more challenging than expected, then the problems of discriminating Soviet warheads from decoys in space will be both geometrically and qualitatively multiplied. The threat scenarios posed by the weapons labs are ten times as great and far more complicated than those generated by SDIO in the summer of 1985.

— Passive discrimination of Soviet warheads from decoys in space may have little military utility. Possible Soviet countermeasures make passive discrimination by itself ineffective. Some progress has been made in research of a new type of discrimination—interactive discrimination. At this point, however, interactive discrimination is little more than an interesting and promising concept.

— SDIO has been incorporating into its plans the findings of its Eastport Study on "Battle Management and Computing," which was sharply critical of the planning priorities that went into the initial development of SDI's defense plans. If a dramatic shift in emphasis from battle hardware to battle management computing is required, current defense system plans might be irrelevant.

— The space shuttle tragedy pointed out current logistical difficulties with the deployment of space-based payloads. Unless fairly dramatic advances are made in U.S. space transportation, logistics and support capabilities, it may be impossible to begin deploying any SDI system until after the year 2000. This raises serious questions about the current schedules and emphases of the program.

(5) After four years, the SDI budget has more than tripled. SDIO has slowed the pace of some of its research efforts; however, this has not been primarily as a result of congressional budget cuts, as SDIO officials have claimed. Decisions to deemphasize certain research efforts seem to be driven by their lack of technical promise (as was the case with chemical lasers), and by SDIO's insistence on keeping to an unrealistic "technology-limited" research schedule.

(6) Public debate on the SDI has often centered on the desirability of performing a robust research program. The authors of this report consider that question moot. Public support for research is broad and bipartisan. The more relevant question involves the pace and direction of this program.

(7) SDI funding levels are as large as the combined armed services' entire technology-based research and development programs. The administration submitted a budget for fiscal year 1987 that would have more than quintupled SDI funding in just four years. Congress, however, cut almost $2 billion out of the administration's FY 1987 request, signaling at the same time its deep skepticism over the president's vision of Star Wars. Meanwhile, SDIO has yet to produce a blueprint of a Star Wars defense which could be tested against a realistic set of Soviet threats.

Chapter 1

SDI Technology and Research

The Strategic Defense Initiative has become the Reagan administration's top defense priority. If carried to fruition, SDI research alone would become the largest military or space program the U.S. has ever undertaken—larger, for example, than the Manhattan Project that developed the first atomic bomb or the Apollo project that placed a man on the moon. Already SDI, though it involves only a small percentage of the total Defense Department budget, has become a formidable endeavor. As now structured, the program consists of some 50 major projects and more than 1,000 defense contracts. A detailed description of the entire SDI research program would require another book, indeed, a very large book. What follows, is a guide to the basic goals of the SDI program and a broad outline of the research being pursued to achieve those goals.

HOW SDI WOULD WORK

The type of technology deployed in a ballistic missile defense (BMD) system largely depends on what areas are to be defended. Least difficult, in terms of the technology that must be developed, would be a limited BMD system protecting only the U.S. strategic land-based missiles based in hardened silos. This is called a "hard-point defense." Indeed, until the Star Wars speech, U.S. BMD research concentrated on defending these missile silos. The technological task becomes greater when the limited defense is

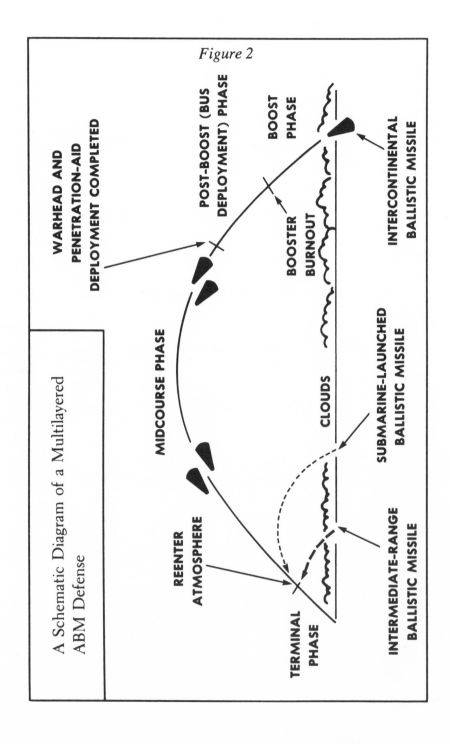

Figure 2

A Schematic Diagram of a Multilayered ABM Defense

expanded to cover other U.S. military targets such as command and control centers, communications facilities, and military bases.

The most difficult BMD system to develop is population defense—that is, defense of all military and civilian targets. This is the defense President Reagan proposes and it is the type of defense SDI is researching. Sometimes called an "area defense" or "SDI defense," it seeks ultimately to erect a *nearly* leakproof shield that would prevent Soviet nuclear weapons from striking any part of the United States.

SDI planners envision this defensive shield—or "architecture," as it is known—as being a series of layers with each layer successively thinning out the offensive nuclear force the Soviets might launch (see Figure 2).

BOOST-PHASE DEFENSE

The first layer would consist of the boost-phase defense, which would attempt to destroy Soviet missiles after they leave their silos, but before their boosters are jettisoned. The boost-phase lasts three to five minutes during which the three-stage booster travels to an altitude of about 200 kilometers then finally burns out.

As will be explained later, the boost-phase presents the best opportunity for strategic defenses to substantially reduce Soviet nuclear forces because (a) a missile with the large bright exhaust plume trailing it can be more easily spotted and tracked by space-based sensors, and (b) destruction of a single missile results in the destruction of multiple warheads and decoys atop it. Although the number of Soviet strategic missiles the boost-phase defense should eliminate would likely be large (the present Soviet force consists of over 1,300 land-based ICBMs and 900 submarine-launched ballistic missiles), the number of targets other layers of the strategic defense would face would be substantially larger if those missiles were allowed to dispense their thousands of decoys and warheads.

POST BOOST-PHASE DEFENSE

After the booster burns out and its last stage is jettisoned, the rest of the missile consists of a post-boost vehicle (PBV) or "bus" packed with the warheads and decoys. This post-boost phase lasts six to ten minutes, during which the bus nearly reaches apogee at about 1,200 kilometers above the earth. During this time, the bus uses its thrusters to adjust its trajectory and with each adjustment releases warheads and decoys that speed toward selected targets.

If the missile cannot be destroyed during the boost phase, the next opportune time is during the post-boost phase before the bus releases its warheads. However, because it is smaller and emits less heat than the booster, the bus alone can be more difficult to detect and destroy.

MIDCOURSE PHASE DEFENSE

The next layer of defense is the midcourse phase, the period after the bus dispenses its warheads and decoys in space and before those objects reenter the earth's atmosphere. The midcourse phase lasts about 20 minutes, depending on the type of missile that fired the warheads.

It is during the midcourse phase that the strategic defense has the most time to find and destroy the warheads, which are speeding along independently toward their targets in the United States. Yet while the defense layer guarding the midcourse phase has more time to engage the enemy than in the boost and post-boost defense layers, it will have much more difficulty finding and destroying the targets. Before the midcourse defense can destroy the Soviet warheads, it must pick them out from among the hundreds of thousands of decoys and bits of debris that will be in space. The warhead also will be more difficult to spot and destroy because it is much smaller, has a harder and thicker skin than a missile booster and will emit and reflect less detectable energy.

TERMINAL PHASE DEFENSE

The final layer of defense occurs at the terminal phase of the warhead's flight. The terminal phase begins when the warhead reenters the atmosphere about 100 kilometers above the United States.

During this phase, the warheads are easier to detect because friction with air molecules in the atmosphere heats them up, while the presumably lighter weight decoys slow down due to air drag and are thus separated from the real warheads.

However, the defense has only tens of seconds to destroy the warheads before they strike their targets. And because the warheads will likely be salvaged fused (that is, set to detonate if anything strikes them along their flight paths), the defense's interception must occur high enough in the atmosphere so the nuclear explosions do not cause unacceptable damage on the ground.

SDI RESEARCH

Each of the independent layers in the defensive system—or systems architecture—must perform five important tasks: (1) surveillance and acquisition to detect and identify enemy targets, (2) discrimination to distinguish the warheads and missiles from decoys and debris, (3) pointing and tracking so each defensive weapon can aim and hit the target, (4) target destruction by the defensive weapons, and (5) kill assessment to ensure that the target has been destroyed.

To accomplish these tasks within the layers and to coordinate the defense among the layers, SDI is pursuing research under five large programs: (1) Surveillance, Acquisition, Tracking and Kill Assessment, (2) Directed Energy Weapons, (3) Kinetic Energy Weapons, (4) Systems Concepts and Battle Management, (5) Survivability, Lethality and Key Support Technologies (see Figure 3 for the funding levels of these programs).

SURVEILLANCE, ACQUISITION, TRACKING & KILL ASSESSMENT

The surveillance program is researching the space- and ground-based sensors that will be needed to (a) detect the enemy attack and sound the warning, (b) discriminate between the attacking objects that are threatening, such as warheads, and those that are not, such as decoys, (c) track the threatening objects so they can be intercepted and destroyed, and (d) confirm that the threatening object in fact has been destroyed. As can be imagined, surveillance becomes a monumental task. Everything that the enemy throws at the defense must be accounted for so nothing slips through.

A number of space-based, space-launched, air-based and ground-based sensors are being researched. They generally fall into three broad technology categories:

(1) passive sensors, which identify and track targets by detecting their naturally occurring emissions. For example, current U.S. early warning satellites detect Soviet missiles launches with infrared sensors that pick up the radiation from the missiles' exhaust plumes;

(2) active sensors, such as ground-based radars, which strike the targets with microwaves or illuminate them, then track what is reflected off them; and

(3) interactive sensors, which jostle a target with a directed energy beam then observe its characteristics with a passive sensor. Interactive sensors, which will be discussed later, are being researched to discriminate warheads from decoys in space.

DIRECTED ENERGY WEAPONS

The directed energy weapons program consists of research into various types of lasers and particle beam weapons. A laser produces a coherent beam of light that may be in the infrared, visible, ultraviolet, or x-ray region of the electromagnetic spectrum. The lasing occurs when more molecules or atoms are in an excited higher energy state and fewer are in a lower energy state. As the excited molecules drop back to a lower energy state they emit radiation. Chemical lasers—such as hydrogen fluoride (HF) and deuterium fluoride (DF)—produce laser radiation through chemical reactions. Excimer lasers use an excited dimmer, or two-atom molecule, whose laser radiation is produced by a pulsed electrical discharge process. Free electron lasers produce an intense beam of radiation by passing a beam of electrons through a magnetic field. X-ray lasers produce their beams by "pumping" a lasant material into an excited state with a nuclear explosion. SDI scientists hope to develop lasers powerful enough and with a sufficient range to destroy targets such as a Soviet missile by burning holes through the missile's skin or delivering what amounts to a shock wave that causes structural damage.

Figure 3
STRATEGIC DEFENSE FUNDING
($ million)

Strategic Defense Initiative Organization			
Program	**FY1985***	**FY1986***	**FY1987***	**FY1988†**
Surveillance, Acquisition, Tracking & Kill Assessment	546.0	857.0	907.0	1,492.7
Directed Energy Weapons	377.6	844.4	826.5	1,103.7
Kinetic Energy Weapons	256.0	595.8	718.5	1,074.7
Systems Concepts & Battle Management	100.3	227.3	379.9	627.3
Survivability, Lethality & Key Support Technologies	108.4	221.6	319.5	900.4
Management HQ, SDI	9.1	13.1	16.0	22.0
Total	1,397.4	2,759.2	3,167.4	5,220.8

Department of Energy			
Program	**FY1985***	**FY1986***	**FY1987***	**FY1988†**
Strategic Defense-Related Programs	224	288	315	569

*Appropriated
†Requested

Particle beam weapons fire subatomic particles at the target instead of electromagnetic radiation. These subatomic particles may be protons, electrons, neutral atoms, heavy ions, or other exotic bits of matter that are accelerated to speed-of-light velocities. The particle beam could pass through a missile's skin and destroy electronic systems inside. Particles that are accelerated with electric fields produce charged beams that will bend in the earth's magnetic field, making them difficult to aim. SDI scientists, therefore, have been investigating neutral particle beams that are not affected by magnetic fields and are easier to aim.

KINETIC ENERGY WEAPONS

Kinetic energy weapons use rockets or projectiles that collide with missiles or warheads at very high speed, destroying them on impact. SDI, for example, is pursuing research into space-based kinetic kill vehicles—rockets fired from orbiting battle stations at Soviet missiles. SDI also is investigating space-based rail guns, which would use electromagnetic launchers to hurl hypervelocity projectiles at Soviet targets. On the ground, high-acceleration rocket interceptors are being researched that would destroy incoming warheads by colliding with them at very high speeds, obviating the need for nuclear explosives.

SYSTEMS CONCEPTS & BATTLE MANAGEMENT

Developing the individual weapons and sensors for a strategic defense is an extremely challenging undertaking. Just as challenging, if not more so, is connecting the thousands of weapons and sensors into a coordinated and effective strategic defense. To pursue this goal, SDI has established a program to investigate various blueprints, or system architectures, for how a total defense might be established.

Furthermore, this program is investigating how the weapons and sensors might be coordinated and controlled in combat through an automated battle management system involving highly sophisticated computer hardware and software.

SURVIVABILITY, LETHALITY & SUPPORT TECHNOLOGIES

A number of other critical technological hurdles must be overcome in order to develop effective weapons and sensors. For example, weapons and sensors that are based in space will have to be "survivable" to successfully fend off countermeasures and counter-defense attacks by the enemy. Ballistic missile defense weapons tend to make even better anti-satellite weapons. SDI, therefore, must find a way to protect its space-based assets from both enemy counter-defensive weapons and defensive weapons.

Most directed energy beams at this point are too weak and have too short a range to be militarily effective. For that reason, this program is conducting lethality research to increase the power in the beams so they can destroy targets. Finally, a massive support infrastructure, which will be discussed in greater detail later, would be needed to deploy and maintain defensive systems. SDI is investigating technologies to accomplish this task in a cost-effective manner.

PHASED PROGRAM

Because of the magnitude of the program the president has proposed, it is difficult for anyone to predict with any accuracy how it might evolve over the next several decades. The SDI Organization has said it envisions the Strategic Defense Initiative proceeding along four general phases. Phase one is the research phase that would last through the early 1990s. During this phase SDI would conduct research on various ballistic missile defense options so a future president could decide whether or not to begin the full-scale engineering development of a defensive system. It is assumed that the Soviets would keep pace with their strategic defense technology program.

Full-scale engineering development would begin in the early 1990s during phase two. Prototypes of the defense system would be designed, built and tested. Such development would abrogate the 1972 ABM Treaty as it is now written. Again, the Soviets would follow suit.

The third phase in the administration's plan is called the transition phase when both the United States and the Soviet Union begin incremental, sequential deployment of their defense systems—that is, limited defenses would be erected first and expanded later. All the while, arms control agreements would be negotiated to reduce drastically both sides' offensive nuclear forces. SDI opponents and proponents agree that the transition phase will be difficult to manage and is fraught with dangers. For example, an extremely destabilizing situation would occur if either side during the transition phase perceived that the other side had jumped ahead in   defensive capabilities.

During phase four, as the SDI Organization projects it, both superpowers reach the president's goal of astrodome shields protecting them. Both sides would be at their fullest deployment of "highly effective"—but not perfect—defenses, while arms control agreements would have reduced both sides' offensive nuclear forces to their lowest level.

SDI FUNDING

The SDI program was based on the recommendations of the Defensive Technologies Study Team (the Fletcher Panel). The Fletcher study laid out a general blueprint for a "technology-limited" research program, which largely became the basis for SDI's future budget submissions.

Strictly defined, a technology-limited program is limited only by technological progress. The Fletcher study recommended that all aspects of SDI research proceed at a pace as fast as the technology would allow, so a future administration and Congress could make a decision by the early 1990s as to whether strategic defenses are feasible and should be developed. On the other hand, a funding-limited program is limited by the funds appropriated. As such, priorities have to be set on the pacing of individual aspects of the research.

SDI requested $1.78 billion for FY1985, $3.72 billion for FY1986, and $4.8 billion for FY1987. For FY1988, SDI requested $5.2 billion, which would make it the largest major weapons program in the entire DoD budget. SDI also has projected a total cost for the research phase of about $33 billion between FY1985 and FY1990, more than double the predicted funding before the president's March 1983 speech. (This figure does not include the hundreds of millions of dollars funded in the Department of Energy for strategic defense-related research.)

SDI will be the largest military research program the Department of Defense has ever undertaken. The research alone will be in excess of the full deployment costs of many major weapons systems. Moreover, at its current level of funding SDI is as expensive as the total technical base research efforts of all the armed services.

SDI officials have avoided placing a price tag on deploying a comprehensive defensive shield. Outside experts, such as former defense secretaries James Schlesinger and Harold Brown, have predicted that a full development and deployment of a strategic defense system would cost as much as $1 trillion.

SDI officials, insisting that the $1 trillion estimate is too high, say it is too early in the research for accurate forecasts of deployment costs. Rather than give an estimate of SDI's total cost based on current information, General Abrahamson said he is working to develop what SDI *should* cost if it is to be affordable and meet the cost-effective-at-the-margin criteria, as posed by the President's principal arms control adviser Ambassador Paul Nitze. Shortly, the SDI organization hopes to begin establishing "cost objectives" for its weapons—for example, $1 million for a ground-based intercepter, according to Abrahamson.

Nevertheless, SDI officials appear to be privately making preliminary estimates of deployment costs based on information accumulated so far. For example, one official projected that a particular defensive architecture (the configuration of weapons in a defensive shield) would cost $350 billion to deploy.

Whatever the final cost, it is clear that the present SDI program is not being funded at the pace the administration had originally envisioned. SDIO has submitted what it considered a technology-limited budget to Congress the past three years. Congress, however, has approved a more funding-limited approach.

In FY1985, the administration requested $1.78 billion for SDI, but Congress appropriated $1.4 billion. For FY1986 SDIO requested $3.7 billion, but received $2.76. For FY1987 the administration requested $4.8 billion for the Defense Department portion of SDI and $603 million for the Department of Energy portion, for a total funding of $5.4 billion. Congress, however, approved a total funding of $3.5 billion.

Actually, it is not accurate to argue that Congress has ever cut SDIO's budget. In fact, Congress allowed SDIO's budget to increase by 41 percent for FY1985, 92 percent for FY1986, and 17 percent for FY1987. Reductions have occurred only in the sense that the Congress has refused to make the increases as large as the administration requested. In fact, Congress has allowed more than a *tripling* of the SDI budget since 1984.

It is also interesting to note that, according to SDI documents, many of the recent cuts were made in demonstration projects, which some critics of the program have worried are moving too far ahead of other, more important research efforts. However, two even more important trends are evident as a result of recent funding shifts in the SDI program.

First, the Fletcher budget is not the budget SDI now has, even though SDI is still clinging to the Fletcher Panel's timeline. As noted above, the Fletcher Panel proposed a technology-limited program, in which every research project was funded as heavily as it could be carried forward, so a decision on whether to develop strategic defenses could be made in the early 1990s. It is unlikely that even with a technology-limited budget and unlimited funding, SDIO could make a sound development decision by that date. However in the absence of unlimited funding, SDIO's managers faced two choices.

They could continue to carry every research project forward, which, under a funding-limited program, would mean that the early 1990s development decision might be deferred to a later date. Or they could set priorities in the program—that is, slow-down some projects, speed-up others—in order to reach a development decision by the early 1990s.

SDIO has chosen the second option. It is making choices among competing research projects and keeping to the same timeline of reaching a development decision in the early 1990s. SDI officials candidly admit that there now will be significantly more risks associated with that development decision as a result of not all critical technologies coming on line by that time. General Abrahamson, for example, spoke of the "risks" incurred as the timeline for experiments slips and as "early" technical decisions are made. The implications of this strategy and its risks will be considered later.

The second trend now evident is that SDI's research priorities are substantially different from the ones proposed by the Fletcher Panel and from the ones made when the FY1985 and FY1986 budget requests were submitted.

SDIO officials claim that congressional budget cuts were to blame for the shifts in priorities. Indeed, a few of the shifts were necessitated because of reduced funding. However, it is clear that some cuts were prompted by a realization that some of the research projects would not prove militarily useful. SDIO has discovered that many of the research projects the Fletcher Panel gave high priority, based on the body of knowledge available at the time, did not in fact merit such priority.

Again, it is interesting to note that these were many of the same projects that critics had contended were over-funded.

Chapter 2

Progress in SDI Research

The SDI organization is justified in claiming that progress has been made the past two years in its research. One should not expect otherwise, considering the large increase in funding for the research. In a very short time, the Department of Defense has organized a vigorous, centrally directed program that is conducting research at a quickening pace.

This research has been focused on reaching a conclusive deployment decision by the early 1990s. Statements from SDI officials that, "this is just a research program at this stage," are not entirely accurate. SDI is not a research program in the traditional sense of one that simply explores new technologies. It is a program aimed at reaching a decision on what kind of defensive system the U.S. could develop in the 1990s and then deploy. The research, therefore, is being driven not necessarily for exploration's sake but rather by that schedule.

ORGANIZATIONAL REALIGNMENT

Progress has been made in SDI research by the very fact that its projects have been consolidated under one organization. Before SDI, each military service had its own missile defense research program. In addition, various DoD agencies pursued research into individual aspects of ballistic missile defense. As a result, U.S. BMD research has lacked a centralized approach.

By bringing together 25 BMD-related programs from the Army, Air Force, Navy, Defense Nuclear Agency, and Defense Advanced Research Projects Agency, SDI has given strategic defense research much more direction and control. Although this study uncovered complaints from the executing agencies about SDI's management, it is generally conceded that the BMD research has more potential for success by having a single organization supervising it.

AN ASSESSMENT OF SUCCESSES

The facilities visited and briefings conducted for this report revealed that numerous research projects under SDI have demonstrated significant progress during the past three years. There is a high degree of professionalism, enthusiasm, and expertise among the scientists and military planners working in the national laboratories and military facilities. There is also a healthy amount of skepticism among these researchers. Hard questions are being asked about SDI, and the research teams are working intensely to find the answers.

For example, Lawrence Livermore Laboratory is making progress in its research on a free electron laser. The SDI Organization envisions that a free electron laser beam would be fired from the ground to a space-based relay mirror, which would direct the beam to a lower orbiting battle mirror, which, in turn, would direct the beam to an approaching enemy missile.

During the past three years SDIO has revised its views considerably on the characteristics its lasers should possess to be militarily useful directed energy weapons. For example, SDIO now believes that short wavelength lasers, which require fewer components in space, would be more militarily effective than space-based chemical lasers. In addition, the free electron laser has advantages over conventional lasers in terms of wavelength tuning, high power capability, good optical quality, and high efficiency.

SDIO's free electron laser program, however, has undergone some "political turbulence," according to the program's scientists. The controversy centered on which of two types of lasers should be emphasized in the SDI program: (1) the radio frequency (RF) linac free electron laser, or (2) the induction linac free electron laser. The initial RF linac free electron laser is being developed by Boeing Company while Los Alamos is conducting theoretical research into a more high-powered version of the laser. Research into the induction linac free election laser at this point is being handled entirely by the Livermore Laboratory. The main difference between the two lasers is the type of accelerator used.

Each laser has advantages and disadvantages. While the controversy surrounding the two lasers is too complex to be fully developed here, serious concerns had been raised in the scientific community that SDIO was prematurely selecting one laser over the other for a large-scale demonstration before the necessary basic research had been completed. The free electron laser program, however, has now stabilized, according to the scientists involved in its research. A selection of the RF or induction laser has been delayed until additional research has been conducted on both concepts and an outside committee has evaluated their merits.

Producing a militarily capable ground-based laser will be a monumental undertaking for SDIO. First a device to produce the laser beam must be built; Los Alamos, Boeing, and Livermore are currently seeking to overcome the numerous technical hurdles. Next a beam control system must be built to receive the laser beam and prepare it for passage through the atmosphere. This will require a sizeable effort. As the atmosphere changes 1,000 times a second, the laser beam passing through the atmosphere will have to be adjusted at least that frequently. A low-energy laser beacon will have to be fired between the relay mirror and the ground-based system to tell it how the atmosphere is changing.

In addition to building the ground-based laser system, SDI also will have to construct the space-based relay and battle mirrors that would take the beam and direct it toward a hostile missile. Developing these mirrors was described by an expert close to the program as "a horrendous problem." SDIO's research into these space-based mirrors, however, has been drastically scaled back for the moment resulting in significant risks for the ground-based laser effort. The risk is that we may have the ground-based portion of a prototype system completed in the mid-1990s but will not have the space-based mirrors ready to complete the system.

No firm dates exist for when a fully capable free electron laser system might be available. In fact, serious questions remain as to whether such a system may ever be available for ballistic missile defense. It may be that the only reasonable role for the free electron laser will be as an antisatellite weapon fired from the ground. SDIO's architecture studies, nevertheless, envision ground-based free electron lasers being available in the next century.

Recognizing that passive sensors will have difficulty discriminating warheads from decoys, Sandia Laboratory is pursuing a promising concept called interactive discrimination. Indeed, it may turn out that particle beam or laser technology will be more valuable as discriminators than as weapons. While interactive discrimination will be addressed later, it should be noted that neutral particle beam weapons have taken on a more important role in the SDI program. SDI scientists are investigating whether they can build a neutral particle beam device that would tap warheads and decoys with a nearby detector device picking up the neutron and gamma ray emissions to discriminate between decoys and heavier warheads.

The SDI program has made considerable progress in developing the accelerator for the neutral particle beam. A linear ion accelerator propels ions to velocities close to the speed of light and then strips the extra electrons off the ions to create neutrally charged particles, which are shot at the target. Building a linear accelerator is not new. Physicists have been constructing them since 1947. Moreover, Sandia scientists reported a recent "breakthrough" when a radio frequency quadrapole was adapted to provide a high quality ion beam for the accelerator. However, building a militarily capable neutral particle beam discriminator or weapon will pose a number of challenges, four of which will be reviewed here.

The first hurdle to achieving a militarily useful system is reducing the weight of a space-based accelerator and detector. Los Alamos scientists believe that the weight must be reduced from

300 metric tons per platform (the current capability that would cost $2 billion to put in space) to a battle-ready platform of just 30 tons.

Second, current rudimentary accelerators on the ground take weeks to start up and then must be constantly fine-tuned by technicians while they are operating. In space, the accelerator must start within a matter of minutes and must be fine-tuned by remote control. Furthermore, the device that supplies the ions to the accelerator is notoriously fickle. Can this ion source be turned on remotely? Will the spacecraft itself become charged electrically and affect the creation of the neutral particle beam?

Third, once the components are constructed in the required scale, piecing them together into an effectively operating discriminator will be "a real problem," according to scientists working on the project.

Fourth, the electrical power requirements to operate the neutral particle beam accelerator are much greater than anything ever supplied in space. Some scientists envision the power being supplied by rocket motors turning turbine generators. There are several unanswered questions: Will hot gases emitted by the rocket motors get in the way of the beam? What sort of vibrations and platform rotations will be caused by these motors? Will they disturb the beam weapon's tracking and pointing accuracy?

Turning to another research effort in directed energy, the Livermore Laboratory's work on X-ray lasers has also shown progress, despite considerable scientific debate over what strategic defense mission such a weapon might preform. As currently envisioned, the X-ray laser would be ground- or sea-based and launched by rocket into space in the event of a Soviet attack. A nuclear bomb on the rocket would detonate in space and just before being vaporized, the laser would convert a small percentage of the extraordinary energy of the nuclear explosion into intense beams of X-rays aimed at multiple targets. As will be discussed later, SDI scientists are now examining the X-ray laser as much for its potential as an antisatellite weapon as they are for its potential as a defensive weapon.

Significant advances also have been made in the research into kinetic energy weapons. SDI's Space-Based Kinetic Kill Vehicle

(SBKKV) Project is investigating placing small rockets on battle stations in space that would be fired at Soviet missiles in the boost phase. In the recently completed Phase I of the project, SDIO succeeded in defining a concept for what a constellation of SBKKVs might look like. The project was able to define the type of experiments it wants to conduct to prove the system's feasibility. Also, some preliminary technology validation experiments were conducted in propulsion and interceptor electronics. The project, however, still has a long way to go before an operational SBKKV is produced. To use a football analogy, the team has had a successful draft and a good first week of spring training, but it's a long way to the Super Bowl.

In the second phase, project managers will try to validate the concepts they defined in the first phase. They will attempt to build portions of the SBKKV battle station and rockets. Then they will try to demonstrate that they can build the entire system by examining and testing its various components. The second phases will culminate with a test of the rocket interceptor technology by 1989-1990. All the while, the project will be further refining its concept of how the entire defensive system of SBKKVs should be produced and deployed. Phase II will be a considerable undertaking as a number of critical issues remain to be resolved before an operational SBKKV could ever be deployed.

The ground-based interceptors that will defend the U.S. in the midcourse and terminal phases of attack are the exoatmospheric reentry vehicle interceptor subsystem (ERIS) and the high endoatmospheric defense interceptor (HEDI). Both systems would be non-nuclear. ERIS would attempt to destroy Soviet warheads in the midcourse phase, while HEDI would attempt to destroy the re-entry vehicles that escaped midcourse defenses and made it to the terminal phase.

The current research for ERIS and HEDI is divided into two phases: (1) the technology validation experiment for each interceptor, aimed at building a prototype model that will be test fired in 1990-1991 to demonstrate critical technology issues; and (2) advanced technology research to produce by the mid-1990s an operational interceptor that is smaller, lighter, less expensive and more capable. The total cost of the validation experiments for both interceptors will be substantial, $794 million for ERIS and $979 million for HEDI. No total cost estimates have been made for the advanced technology research.

ERIS, which is being developed by the Lockheed Missile and Space Company, represents the most mature ground-based interceptor technology on the SDI drawing boards. Already, the Army has tested a very crude prototype model, the 1984 Homing Overlay Experiment (HOE), which gave SDI officials some confidence that incoming warheads could be destroyed with non-nuclear interceptors. In fact, SDI officials have gone so far as to claim that HOE demonstrated that strategic defenses will work. This was hardly the case. The HOE was far too heavy for operational purposes. The kill vehicle alone weighed over one ton, while an ERIS kill vehicle should weigh about 100 pounds. HOE vehicles cost over $10 million apiece, while SDIO hopes to get the cost of each ERIS down to less than $1 million. HOE had delicate, sensitive instruments that required tremendous precision while an operational ERIS must have rugged, reliable instruments with medium precision. Maintaining HOE in an operational state would be a "staggering thought," according to one Lockheed engineer. ERIS must be a quick-launch, easy-to-operate system.

The HEDI program is not as far along as the ERIS program. In fact, while the 1984 Homing Overlay Experiment demonstrated the feasibility of an interceptor destroying a warhead in the midcourse phase, we will not demonstrate the feasibility of destroying that warhead with a non-nuclear interceptor within the atmosphere in the terminal phase until 1989.

In a number of other projects, SDI scientists have discovered that technical requirements for a particular system will not be as difficult as once thought; in other instances, they have discovered that technical requirements will be more complicated. For example, Sandia Laboratory is making significant progress in defining potential Soviet countermeasures and the survivability requirements for a U.S. defensive system.

The SDI organization also has made progress in identifying both research that they believe will not likely have much military utility and research that is more critical to the success of a strategic defense system. SDI briefers avoided stating that some research is being de-emphasized because it lacks military utility. Nevertheless, it is clear SDI now believes that certain research projects, such as space-based chemical lasers or hypervelocity launchers, are lesser candidates at the moment. SDI officials also recognize that progress in other research, such as survivability of space-based assets and midcourse discrimination, is critical to an effective defense (although publicly SDI directors hedge as to how critical they are).

Finally, it appears that a number of small projects among the more than 1,000 contracts SDI has let so far have yielded results. From tiny gyroscopes to computer chip technology, a number of ideas and innovative technologies have surfaced from universities and small businesses as a result of SDI.

Success, however, in one small project—or hundreds of projects, for that matter—does not necessarily make for a successful strategic defense program. The task at hand and the hurdles it faces are so exacting that the sum of research cannot be judged solely by its parts.

Any meaningful assessment of SDI research, therefore, has to be made of the program in its entirety. In other words, the bottom-line question is: Overall, what kind of progress has SDI made in its research? What do all the individual research projects and initiatives add up to?

Has SDI made amazing progress, as senior administration officials have claimed? Have there been major breakthroughs? Has SDI research advanced so dramatically that the question of strategic defense's technical feasibility is already settled?

After interviewing more than 100 scientists, engineers, defense experts and military officials deeply involved in SDI's research, the authors of this study have concluded that the simple answer to these questions is: no. Granted, each person interviewed for this study spoke from his own perspective and therefore could not speak for the entire program. Nevertheless, taken together their assessments lead us to the conclusion that SDI research has not progressed nearly as rapidly as has been portrayed by senior administration and SDI officials.

Contrary to press reports, there have been no incredible breakthroughs in SDI research. There has been progress, to be sure. But key SDI scientists interviewed for this study agreed that their results were not as spectacular as has been portrayed to the media. If anything, these working scientists resented the fact that the progress of their research has been inflated, because it undermines their credibility as scientists. As one researcher said, the hyping of the progress "is driving good people out of the program."

Contrary to claims by administration officials and SDI's top leadership, the program's scientists and military planners across the country have *not* concluded that SDI is militarily and economically feasible. They presently have little idea whether it is. The fact is, they are still assembling the research to ask and answer the right questions.

If anything, the dramatic progress SDI has achieved during the past two years has been in identifying the operational problems a strategic defense system would face. The research being accumulated by SDI clearly indicates that the technological hurdles are much greater, the possible Soviet offensive threat and countermeasures would be much more formidable, and logistical and battle management difficulties are much more complex than originally envisioned. Figure 4 summarizes some of the hurdles as some scientists at the Sandia laboratory presently see them.

Figure 4
STRATEGIC DEFENSE IN A NUTSHELL

- BOOST PHASE
  - Might be Feasible if Survivable
  - If not Survivable, Depend on Midcourse and Terminal
- MIDCOURSE PHASE
  - Might be Feasible if Discrimination is Solvable
  - If not, Depend on Boost and Terminal
- TERMINAL PHASE
  - Overwhelmed without Boost or (and?) Midcourse for Population Defense
  - Maybe can Stand Alone for Hard Target Defense

Source: Sandia National Laboratories

Chapter 3

Emerging Problems

The Strategic Defense Initiative began as a result of a top-down decision process. That is, President Reagan, with little or no consultation with the Defense Department, the State Department, the Congress, or U.S. allies, decided in March 1983 to launch a massive SDI research program. This process has been criticized because, some believe, the president should have first consulted his best experts in the Departments of Defense and State, sounded out Congress, and consulted our allies before he ever made his famous Star Wars speech. The president's supporters, however, have maintained that if Reagan had done all that, the SDI program would have never gotten off the ground. The president's vision would have been strangled by bureaucratic inertia, congressional opposition, and Allied timidity. It was far better, they contended, to have the bold stroke of the March 1983 speech to launch the program.

Whatever the advisability of the process that Reagan pursued, it was clear that his approach resulted in the SDI Organization having to scramble in order to catch up with the decision. Since its inception, therefore, the SDI Organization has devoted considerable time and energy to analyzing the hurdles that it faces in pursuing the president's vision.

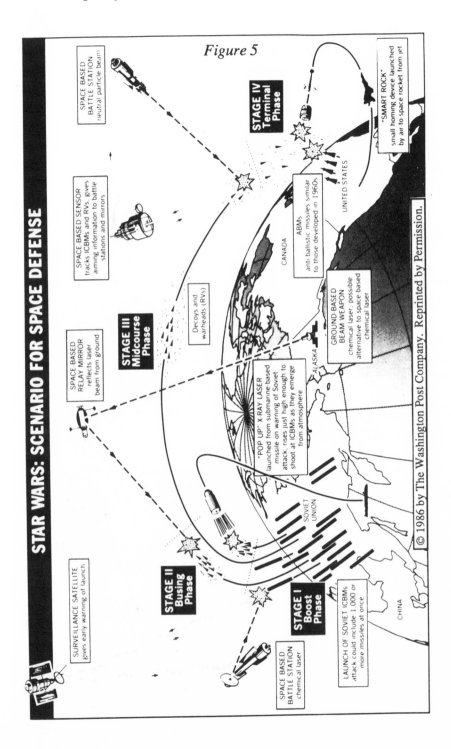

Figure 5

STAR WARS: SCENARIO FOR SPACE DEFENSE

SPACE BASED BATTLE STATION neutral particle beam

STAGE IV Terminal Phase

"SMART ROCK" small homing device launched by air to space rocket from jet

SPACE BASED SENSOR tracks ICBMs and RVs, gives aiming information to battle stations and mirrors

ABMs anti-ballistic missiles similar to those developed in 1960s

CANADA

UNITED STATES

SPACE BASED RELAY MIRROR reflects laser beam from ground

STAGE III Midcourse Phase

Decoys and warheads (RVs)

GROUND-BASED BEAM WEAPON chemical laser, possible alternative to space based chemical laser

ALASKA

"POP UP" X-RAY LASER launched from submarine based missile on warning of Soviet attack, rises just high enough to shoot at ICBMs as they emerge from atmosphere

SOVIET UNION

SURVEILLANCE SATELLITE gives early warning of launch

STAGE II Busing Phase

STAGE I Boost Phase

LAUNCH OF SOVIET ICBMs attack could include 1,000 or more missiles at once

CHINA

SPACE BASED BATTLE STATION chemical laser

MAKING THE BOOST-PHASE EFFECTIVE

SDI's leadership believes that destroying Soviet missiles in their boost phase—that is, during the first few minutes after launch while the boost rocket is still firing and is easy to detect from space and before the missile dispenses its bus of warheads and decoys—is the most important opportunity for thinning out the Soviet offensive force. Because of the short attack times, a boost-phase defense system must rely on space-based platforms firing rockets, projectiles, or directed energy weapons at the rising booster rockets or on relaying a laser beam fired from the ground.

General Abrahamson made it clear in his briefing that the boost-phase intercept simply must work. While not impossible to achieve, a strategic defense without boost-phase interception would make the entire system much more costly and complicated. "We need the boost phase," Abrahamson emphasized. The briefing charts he and his program managers presented reiterated this point by stating that the "performance of the boost phase intercept tier is critical," and that the "low-leakage, boost-phase intercept is essential."

President Reagan, in conceiving his proposal for a strategic defense, apparently recognized the need for a boost phase defense. He noted that in formulating his proposal one of the first questions he posed to the Joint Chiefs of Staff was whether "it would be worthwhile to see if we could not develop a weapon that could perhaps take out, as they left their silos, those nuclear missiles. And the Joint Chiefs said that such an idea, they believed, was worth researching."

From its inception SDI has been primarily billed by the President as a non-nuclear defense of populations, which would make nuclear weapons impotent and obsolete. Some argue that this would require the deployment of a leak-proof shield. SDI's supporters, as previously noted, respond that an effective defense, generally defined in the 80-90 percent range, would provide the United States with the technological leverage to deter a Soviet missile attack and to move the U.S.S.R. away from further development of what the president has referred to as the "fast movers"—the intercontinental ballistic missiles (ICBMs).

On its face, the argument for technological leverage has some appeal. However, such technological leverage still requires the deployment of a layered defense at least 80 percent effective. (The requirement could be and probably is higher.)

To achieve a system that effective, it is critical that the boost-phase defense layer work. It is in those first few minutes of missile flight, before the bus dispenses its warheads, that the strategic defense can exercise its greatest control. Once the warheads have been released, the problems of strategic defense increase geometrically and the advantage gradually shifts to the offense.

There appears, however, to be some disagreement developing over the importance of the boost-phase and this disagreement may well prove central to the debate over the future feasibility of SDI.

One of the designs presented to SDIO envisions no space-based, boost-phase intercept at all. Instead ground-based, "pop-up" interceptors and directed energy weapons would attack the incoming missiles during the post-boost and midcourse phases (they could not be activated quickly enough to strike during the boost-phase). Some SDI scientists believe that a strategic defense might be successful even if it operated only in the midcourse and terminal phases. (Figure 5 depicts boost-phase, midcourse and ground-based defense schemes).

However there is one very significant problem with an affordable, non-nuclear strategic defense that relies only on the midcourse and terminal layers. That problem is the "discrimination" or location of *attacking* Soviet reentry vehicles amidst decoys during the midcourse phase.

DISCRIMINATION

With the successful demonstration of the 1984 Homing Overlay Experiment, in which a ground-based missile intercepted a reentry vehicle in space, the Army demonstrated that "a bullet could hit a bullet." However, that accomplishment, as significant as it was, pales in comparison with the enormously complicated problem of the bullet *finding* the real bullet.

The problem of discrimination (and target acquisition) is one of distinguishing Soviet warheads from the decoys—and in the midcourse phase of defense it is the most critical technological hurdle SDI officials face. Of course, strategic defense planners could simply ignore discrimination in the midcourse phase and shoot at every incoming target. This option, however, does not appear promising at the moment, considering the potentially huge number of warheads and decoys involved. Therefore, SDI officials have said they will have to emphasize discrimination in this phase of the defense even though the midcourse discrimination hurdle has two very formidable aspects, according to one Sandia scientist: there may be too many warheads and decoys, and the warheads may be indistinguishable from decoys.

PROLIFERATED THREAT

During the past three years, every new SDI assessment of the Soviet's ability to place warheads and decoys in space appears to be different from the previous one; the latest assessment invariably finds the Soviets substantially more capable than the earlier assessment. For example, in the early days of SDI, its researchers claimed the Soviets would only be capable of launching tens of thousands of warheads and decoys. SDI officials also insisted that development of fast-burn boosters to counter boost-phase defenses would reduce the Soviet capability to increase its numbers of warheads and decoys.

In FY1985 that assessment changed somewhat. Sandia scientists reported that fast-burn boosters would not necessarily reduce the weight that could be lifted into space. The briefings received during this study, however, revealed a more ominous picture of the Soviet's ability to complicate midcourse discrimination. Livermore's scientists concluded that fast-burn boosters not only did not reduce the Soviet capability to put warheads and decoys in space, but their fast-burn boosters might even be able to dispense several mini-buses of warheads (instead of a single bus, as is now done), further complicating the post-boost-phase defense.

The first step in discrimination is assembling data on the actual Soviet reentry vehicles (RVs) and using that information to create the means for detecting decoys. Decoys would have different physical characteristics than warheads. In order to tell the difference between a speeding decoy and a speeding warhead, one first has to know what the warhead looks like. At this point, the U.S. is only beginning to collect the midcourse discrimination information it needs on the Soviet warheads because there are so many varieties of them. Also, what the U.S. sees today in Soviet RV test flights might be different from what it would see in war. Meanwhile, the Soviets are presumed to have a better data base on U.S. warheads because ours are more similar to each other.

Because of the types of decoys the Soviets might use to deceive the defense and the nuclear environment they might create by detonating warheads in space, SDI scientists and General Abrahamson himself have concluded that *passive discrimination* alone will not be effective in midcourse phase. (Passive discriminators, such as infrared sensors, attempt to identify objects by detecting their naturally occurring emissions.) Some projects, such as the Space Surveillance and Tracking System (SSTS), have been downgraded because they depend on passive discrimination.

As a result of the anticipated problems with passive discrimination, SDI has turned to the concept of *interactive discrimination.* In this concept low-power lasers or particle beams would be fired at objects in the midcourse to produce observable changes in them, whereupon passive sensors would compare the changes to sort out the warheads from the decoys.

A question remains, however, as to why some SDI projects dealing with passive sensors continue at such a high funding level if the general conclusion is that these sensors would be ineffective. For example, SDI will spend $380 million to demonstrate in early 1989 the Airborne Optical Adjunct (AOA), which uses a passive, long-wave infrared sensor aboard a Boeing 767 jet to detect warheads and decoys in the late midcourse and early terminal phases. Sandia scientists believe that AoA's sensor would have significant problems discriminating warheads from decoys in a nuclear environment. SDI's program manager for sensors insisted, however, that AOA would be valuable for the detection and tracking that is needed before more sophisticated discrimination is required.

Whatever final discrimination technology proves useful, it appears that an effective boost-phase defense is still critical to achieving effective discrimination. It is critical that a boost-phase defense thin out the number of warheads and decoys, with which the midcourse discrimination system must deal. Some SDI officials, therefore, have concluded that a strategic defense minus the boost phase—that is, based only on the midcourse and terminal phases—would likely be overwhelmed by the large number of Soviet warheads and decoys.

SURVIVABILITY

With boost-phase intercept presently recognized as the linchpin for a successful defense system, SDI researchers have concluded that the ultimate problem space-based battle stations will face is survivability. Space-based directed and kinetic energy weapons systems or laser relay stations have tremendous technological and engineering hurdles to cross just to become operational in a non-military environment. But these hurdles pale compared to operating and surviving in a military environment.

Figure 6 provides a sampling of Soviet threats and countermeasures (which the U.S.S.R. would have to pay a high price to deploy) that could affect the survivability or effectiveness of our space-based equipment They include anti-satellite (ASAT) weapons, ground-based lasers, electronic countermeasures, space mines, X-ray lasers, pellets in orbit, and para-military operations. As one senior SDI official stated in a briefing, "We've thought of more threats [to survivability] than even our critics have come up with." For example, every Soviet warhead the bus dispenses becomes a potential ASAT weapon if it is designed to explode near a space platform. Furthermore, the technology required to produce an effective ASAT weapon in most instances is less complicated than the technology needed to produce an effective ABM weapon.

In the past, SDI officials have talked of establishing "keep-out zones" to ward off ASAT's and space mines. The U.S. would declare a certain area around a satellite—say, hundreds or thousands of kilometers—off limits. Anything entering the keep-out zone would be destroyed. Much like the law of the high seas, "rules of the road" would be established in space, which would define what would be considered threatening to U.S. space vehicles and thus subject to attack.

Keep-out zones, however, create countless headaches for military planners and diplomats. First, the 1967 Outer Space Treaty, which declares that no nation can claim sovereignty over outer space, likely would have to be changed and rules of the road negotiated. Second, with thousands of U.S. systems in space and presumably with thousands of Soviet space-based systems in a similar strategic defense, and with each U.S. and Soviet satellite having its own keep-out zone, space will likely become so crowded that there would be little room for satellites to maneuver. Third, ambiguous behavior would greatly complicate enforcement of keep-out zones. Is an intruder a straying satellite or a threatening ASAT? There would also be considerable opportunity for deception, such as hiding space mines or nuclear devices on what are ostensibly commercial space vehicles.

Figure 6
Some Soviet Threats and Countermeasures to SDI

Anti-satellite weapons	Ground-based lasers
Electronic countermeasures	X-ray lasers
Space mines	Pellets in orbit
Para-military forces	Proliferation
Depressed trajectories	Clustering ICBM launches
Booster hardening, spinning	Fast-burn boosters
Quick PBV release	Maneuvering
Salvage fusing	Penetration aids
Decoys	Anti-simulation
Masked warheads	Saturation attack

In our briefings, we asked repeatedly how our space-based units would be protected from Soviet space mines. We never received a plausible answer.

A number of survivability measures are being considered, such as hardening satellites so they can withstand attack, making them maneuverable to evade attack, giving them a protective "shoot-back" capability, or proliferating the defense system with more satellites and decoys. However, SDI studies show that all these efforts to deal with possible Soviet countermeasures pose severe problems.

In order to provide a space-based station with a protective shield (or "harden it"), make it maneuverable, and give it a counter-attack capability, Sandia scientists said that at a minimum its weight and size would have to be doubled. The U.S. would have considerable difficulty lifting this much weight into space. The U.S. also would have difficulty adding many additional satellites, according to one senior SDI official, because it would be too expensive. Also, if the Soviet defense system develops the ability to discriminate between a warhead and decoy, it likely will be capable of discriminating between defensive weapons and decoy satellites.

No doubt there will be other survivability measures—preferential defense of satellites, for example—which would not be as difficult to accomplish. However, at this point survivability research is in its infancy. What follows is a sampling of some of the countermeasures that might be deployed against a U.S. defensive system:

Particle Beams & X-ray Lasers. Because it is impractical to shield against neutral particle beams in space, some SDI officials believe the most difficult survivability problem the U.S. would face is Soviet neutral particle beam weapons, which might destroy our satellites or other space units vital to the defense system. As one SDI official described it, a future scenario in which both the U.S. and the U.S.S.R. deployed neutral particle beam weapons in their defenses with an anti-satellite capability would create a situation something like "the re-enactment of the 'Shootout At the OK Corral.'" He who shoots first, wins.

Pop-up X-ray lasers also present an ASAT threat. A "pop-up" system would consist of nuclear explosive-driven X-ray lasers mounted on ballistic missiles. These missiles would be positioned near the Soviet Union—perhaps in submarines offshore—and would be launched rapidly upon notification of a Soviet attack. Once in space, these devices would fire laser beams at the oncoming Soviet missiles. However, one of the biggest problems with the U.S. deployment of a defensive pop-up X-ray laser is the Soviets' deployment of pop-up X-ray lasers as a counter-defense measure. "The SDI [system] ought to take into consideration the existence of a crude Soviet X-ray laser, and I think SDI has done this," one Livermore scientist said. But he also warned that it is possible the Soviets could have a crude X-ray laser developed by 1995. Match a very crude X-ray laser against a very sophisticated space-based battle station and "the X-ray laser wins every time," he added. Even 1,000 kilometers away, an X-ray laser beam is still so powerful that it is not economical to shield the battle station. The only way to defeat an X-ray laser, according to this scientist, is to either hide from it or to orbit more battle stations than the laser can shoot down.

ASATs and Decoys. Scientists at Los Alamos said they believed the Soviets would respond to U.S. space defenses by attacking the platforms in space. As a matter of fact, Sandia's scientists indicated that in the initial pilot SDI system study it was assumed that the Soviets would react mainly with defense suppression efforts such as direct-ascent anti-satellite weapons (ASAT's). The Soviets might build nuclear-tipped, direct-ascent, anti-satellite interceptors *with decoys* to overwhelm U.S. space platforms, even if the platforms tried to shoot back.

Thus, the discrimination problem, which has previously been described as a midcourse-only problem, could well become a boost-phase problem. Space-based kinetic kill vehicles, for example, would need interactive discriminators to pick out the real ASAT warheads from the decoys.

Nuclear Blasts. One potential countermeasure mentioned frequently in our briefings was the use of successive nuclear blasts in space to blind infrared sensors and possibly destroy key satellites. Before an attack, the Soviets would explode in space a succession of one-megaton blasts every second or so. The director of SDI's Kinetic Energy Weapons Program conceded that this countermeasure to blind sensors was a significant problem.

Fast-Burn Boosters. Another Soviet countermeasure SDI scientists are studying intensively is fast-burn boosters: ICBM rockets that are so fast a space-based system would not have time to engage and attack the missiles. Presently the Soviet SS-18 has a giant, slow booster rocket that requires nearly 300 seconds of burn time, during which it is easy to spot from space using infrared sensors. Space-based defenses, therefore, would have a relatively long time to attack the SS-18. However even before President Reagan's "Star Wars" speech, scientists at Livermore were studying how a Soviet fast-burn booster would complicate strategic defenses that used space-based chemical lasers. Similarly, Livermore scientists have examined how Soviet fast-burn boosters would complicate a defensive system based on space-based kinetic kill vehicles (SBKKV's), that is, space-based rocket interceptors. Livermore's studies came to disturbing conclusions regarding the SBKKV's. One scientist familiar with the studies said: "There is no doubt that for today's [Soviet] SS-18 and SS-24, today's chemical rockets can kill them. The issue is where do you go from there? What's the legacy?" While the SBKKV does a "great job" against the current SS-18, "it fails *catastrophically* for the fast-burn booster," Livermore scientists concluded.

Some scientists at the Los Alamos lab argued that even if the SBKKV cannot hit the Soviet rocket in the boost phase, it could still hit the bus carrying the warheads in the post-boost phase. General Abrahamson has argued that the Soviet bus is still warm enough to be tracked after the booster rocket burns out. However, a scientist at Los Alamos pointed out that the bus after burnout is two to three orders of magnitude dimmer a target than before the burnout so, while the target may not be cold, its emissions are far fainter after booster burnout. The scientist added that the defense has to know where to look for the bus; and if the defense loses the location of the bus, it probably cannot find it again.

Regardless of how bright the bus is, the Livermore analysis argued that against a fast-burn booster the SBKKV will not be effective against the booster or the post-boost bus. A scientist at the Sandia lab who specialized in space survivability also concluded that even if a SBKKV system could shoot back at defense suppression threats, it would not be effective against fast-burn or very-fast-burn, direct-ascent ASATs.

The question then becomes, how long would it take the Soviets to build fast-burn boosters with multiple warheads? It would not be an easy task. If the booster burns out at too low an altitude, when the decoys and reentry vehicles are launched the thin atmosphere at the edge of space will create atmospheric drag, separating the lighter decoys from the heavier warheads. Livermore's scientists, however, discussed a technique one contractor is studying to develop a fast-burn booster and bus that gets the decoys and warheads to a sufficient altitude to avoid atmospheric drag.

Despite the problems the Soviets would have producing them, "the community-wide consensus is that a fast-burn booster is a credible near-term threat," according to one Livermore scientist. A Sandia scientist also pointed out that the Soviet SS-13, while not a fast-burn booster, is a solid propellant rocket that burns in about half the time of an SS-18, and the SS-13 is 1970s technology the Soviets have already deployed. "You can't argue they can't do it," he said, "they did."

Attrition Attacks. The survivability of space-based elements in wartime is only one difficulty; they also have to survive in peacetime. For example, one nagging problem for SDI officials is the possibility of peacetime attacks that gradually diminish the U.S.'s space-based system. A few U.S. satellites occasionally could be rendered inoperative, perhaps by ground-based lasers, with the Soviets denying any responsibility, claiming that the satellites were defective. Or, what if the Soviets, ignoring their treaty obligations, declare the space over the U.S.S.R. a keep-out zone and threaten to shoot down any infringing U.S. BMD battle station? Since deployment of a U.S. defense system would have to be phased to ultimately achieve a comprehensive population defense system, could the Soviets delay deployment of enough segments of the defensive system so that it was unable to fend off countermeasures?

This assessment of survivability problems is not exhaustive. There are many more difficulties and complications involved in deploying space-based defenses capable of withstanding attacks from the offense.

What is the current overall assessment on survivability? At this point, it appears bleak. Scientists at the Sandia Laboratory who have been studying this question intensely have come to the conclusion that space-based, boost-phase defenses can *never* be made survivable, unless by treaty. Boost-phase defenses will never be survivable unless the U.S. and U.S.S.R. agree to certain rules of the road and deployment restrictions defined in arms control agreements. However, in the same breath, these scientists point out that it is wishful thinking (or a myth, as Figure 7 argues) to believe that survivability can be insured by arms control treaties. As one SDI scientist said, if the space-based system "doesn't work on its own, it won't work with arms control."

If space-based defenses are not survivable with arms control or cannot have survivability built in, it does not leave too many appealing options for boost-phase defense. For example, one Sandia scientist has proposed solving the survivability problem by deploying U.S.-Soviet space battle stations that would be built *jointly* by both superpowers and by prearrangement would shoot down ASATs or missiles launched by either side. The scheme, which has been dubbed MIMAS for Mutually Implemented Mutually Assured Survival, may be an elegant technological solution to the survivability problem. But at this point, it is difficult to imagine any type of a joint political arrangement that might permit this kind of operation.

Not surprisingly, SDI's program and project managers who supervise space-based weapons activities are optimistic that the survivability question can be overcome. Some admit, however, that solutions to certain aspects of the survivability dilemma (for example, protecting transition-phase deployment) will have to be accomplished with arms control agreements.

Figure 7
STRATEGIC DEFENSE MYTH # 1

Deficiencies/Vulnerabilities in the Defense Can be Offset by Complimentary Arms Control Agreements

Examples: "Rules of the Road"
Space Keep-Out Zones
Prohibitions on:
Nukes in Space
X-Ray Lasers
Fast Burn Boosters
Penetration Aids
Etc.

Source: Sandia National Laboratories

The Sandia Laboratory findings pose grave questions for the direction and possibilities of current SDI research. Billions of dollars are being pumped into research on space-based weapons systems, but the Sandia findings suggest that this money might well be wasted. Furthermore, *if boost-phase defense is as critical to the success of the entire system as SDIO's leadership presently thinks it is, serious questions need to be asked—and asked early— as to whether a comprehensive strategic defense is really feasible.*

It is also obvious from this discussion that one area requiring much more detailed analysis is the nature of the threat that strategic defenses in space would face. The analysis should be made not just of the Soviet threat projected for today or the next decade, but also the threat the Soviets might pose into the 21st century when a strategic defense might be deployed.

DIRECTION OF SDI PROGRAM

The second major problem concerns the direction the SDI program is taking. This direction, which impacts heavily on the management of the research effort, has many aspects which are categorized below.

SHIFTING PRIORITIES

The current SDI program is substantially different from the one proposed by the Fletcher Panel or projected in the early budget submissions. By some counts, almost half of SDI's projects in 1986 had been given lower priorities, reorientated, or given new missions. A good example of these changes can be found in the Directed Energy Weapons Program.

At the beginning of 1985, SDI officials proposed a three-year budget of more than $1 billion to research space-based chemical lasers in order to conduct a major demonstration project in the early 1990s. Critics at the time questioned the advisability of pumping so much money into this research and an early demonstration project, considering that space-based chemical lasers would have operational limitations, plus problems of surviving in space and attacking missiles during the boost phase. Nevertheless, SDIO insisted that such lasers would be a valuable weapon for the boost-phase segment and an accelerated program to demonstrate them was justified.

Today the space-based chemical laser project has fallen from favor. Its FY86 budget was cut in half from the $348 million requested at the beginning of 1985. Congressional budget cuts were not responsible for the shift in emphasis away from the project; rather, SDI officials have come to realize that their critics were correct. There was too much evidence that space-based chemical laser weapons had serious limitations that rendered them militarily ineffective.

Other directed energy weapons projects have had their missions changed. In 1985, neutral particle beam (NPB) technology was being actively pursued as a space-based weapon. SDI officials by 1986 realized neutral particle beams would have severe hurdles to overcome as a BMD weapon in the near term, so a lower-powered version is being pursued for interactive discrimination. The same verdict is being given for X-ray lasers, whose only near-term mission would be midcourse discrimination. Figure 8 depicts the new roles for directed energy projects in the near term. Two years ago, most of the emphasis in the Directed Energy Weapons Program was on developing directed energy *weapons*. This emphasis has changed. Directed energy technology for interactive discrimination has been given equal emphasis with directed energy weapons research.

The SDI Organization should be commended for recognizing problems in certain technologies and in shifting its priorities. Indeed, by its very nature, a research and development program is expected to be constantly changing. Furthermore, SDIO should exercise a certain degree of management freedom and flexibility to respond to technological evolution and delays. But the dramatic changes that have come about in SDIO's program in the past two years pose a unique set of problems for Congress.

Figure 8
New Applications for Directed Energy Weapons

Technology	Basing Mode	Application	
		Near Term	Far Term
Free electron laser	Ground- or space-based	Midcourse discrimination	Boost-phase, post-boost phase, midcourse discrimination
Neutral particle beam	Space-based	Midcourse discrimination	Midcourse discrimination
HF chemical laser	Space-based	Midcourse discrimination	Boost-phase, post-boost phase, midcourse discrimination
RP excimer laser	Ground -based	Midcourse discrimination	Boost-phase, post-boost phase, midcourse discrimination
X-ray laser	Pop-up	Midcourse discrimination	Midcourse discrimination, boost-phase

Source: Unclassified SDI briefing chart.

Unlike any research project the U.S. has ever undertaken, SDI is intensive, heavily funded, schedule-driven research being conducted not just to explore technology but to decide by the early 1990s what systems are feasible for development and deployment. Priority status for a particular project means hundreds of millions, even billions, of dollars worth of funding. For example, one midcourse discrimination experiment, described as a high priority because it will test a neutral particle beam accelerator in space, may cost up to $1 billion. Several other one-time experiments will cost hundreds of millions of dollars each, according to SDI officials.

In 1985, Congress was asked to appropriate hundreds of millions of dollars for priority projects, many of which were no longer priorities a year later. In 1986 and 1987, Congress was asked to appropriate hundreds of millions of dollars for a different set of priorities. Congress should be concerned about these changes for two reasons.

First, the dramatic shifts in priorities clearly indicate that SDI research, contrary to public pronouncements, is still at a very early stage. SDI officials, despite more than a tripling of their budget, have gained relatively little hard evidence regarding which technologies will result in a feasible, affordable, and survivable comprehensive missile defense. At this point, they are making only educated guesses at what the defensive system might look like.

Congress, therefore, should evaluate carefully the SDI priorities and the hundreds of millions of dollars of funding they entail. Moreover, a degree of skepticism is warranted regarding claims that particular projects have tremendous potential and deserve priority funding.

Second, the SDI priorities Congress is being asked to fund today may change again tomorrow. As one SDI official pointed out, "there are opportunities for major technological breakthroughs for any of the projects we've down-selected." A technology presently not considered as militarily useful may well move to the head of the line in the future.

SDI's Panel on Computing in Support of Battle Management, appointed to consider the computing requirements for strategic defense, concluded in its 1985 Eastport Study that the Phase I architecture designs incorrectly "treated the battle management computing resources and software as part of a system that could be easily and hastily added." The designs, the study continued, were developed "around the sensors and weapons and have paid only 'lip service' to the structure of the software that must control and coordinate the entire system."

The designs (or architectures) should have been driven more by the requirements of battle management, according to the Eastport Study. As a result of this study's recommendations, which called for a strategic defense system "less dependent on tight coordination," some of the weapons and sensors given high priority in the Phase I architectures may well be given a lesser priority. *In other words, the Eastport Study conclusions indicate that the architecture studies would have to be redone to account for the special requirements of battle management computing.*

So far, it has been easy for the SDIO to shift resources to accommodate these changes. But as the total funding level increases, as contracts mature, and as hardware is produced, it will not be as easy to shift funding to new priorities. In other words, the days of easily recovering from premature priorities are nearing an end. Furthermore by rushing toward early technology demonstration projects, SDI officials may well end up with a number of premature choices and Congress may waste a lot of tax dollars. Congress, therefore, should consider the merits of an SDI program oriented toward basic and applied research, which is conducted at a measured pace and is not forced prematurely to establish priorities.

SCHEDULE-DRIVEN RESEARCH

As noted earlier, the SDI organization in 1986 decided to adhere to the same decision timeline established in the technology-limited budget it initially proposed, even though Congress had provided for less funding. As a result, SDI officials freely admitted that there would be more risks associated with the early 1990s development decision than if they received the funds they had requested.

Since there is little chance that Congress will make up for past funding cuts or appropriate all that SDI has requested for FY1988 and future years, a closer look must be given to the risks entailed by remaining with an early 1990s decision date. The following are some of the problems created by the 1990s decision deadline:

(1) Because of funding cutbacks, and the discovery in some cases that the technological hurdles are greater than first thought, many critical systems will not be ready for a development decision by the early 1990s. Because of the inadequacies of passive discrimination and the relative newness of interactive technologies, SDI may not be prepared for a development decision on midcourse discrimination by that time. It therefore is likely that a development decision in the early 1990s would involve not only substantial risks, but also significant gaps in information.

(2) Because an early 1990s development decision would be based on incomplete research, the chances are great that poor choices may be made. At the very least, SDIO will be committing itself to technologies that are in hand or more developed (such as space-based kinetic kill vehicles) but which have limited growth potential (e.g., against Soviet fast-burn boosters).

Moreover, a chief researcher at Livermore Laboratory expressed concern that schedule-driven research might result in a "series of sleazy stunts" rather than well thought-out experiments. As he pointed out, the objective of research is not success but increased knowledge. The pressure to achieve successes will ultimately result in lowering the level of the research.

The Eastport Study also expressed concern that a "time-driven choice for a specific strategic defense architecture" might lock SDI into a defense system that future computers and software would not be able to manage. While shifting priorities may be a relatively painless at the moment, early 1990s development decisions will be difficult and expensive to alter.

(3) The development decision for technologies still projected to come on line by the early 1990s could be more complex and subjective than some realize. Take, for example, space-based kinetic energy weapons, SDI's only near-term deployment option at the moment for the boost-phase. By the early 1990s, this project will only be capable of completing "near-term validation experiments," according to the then-Kinetic Energy Weapons (KEW) program manager, instead of a single demonstration of the technology.

These validation experiments will consist of many subtests, which, when taken together, will supposedly demonstrate the feasibility of space-based KEWs. Decision-makers in the early 1990s thus will be shown different experiments, simulations, and modeling where experiments could not be conducted, and "different pieces of information," according to the program manager, and from all this a "straightforward decision to go into full-scale development will be made." The program manager conceded that subjectivity will be a factor in the decision. "There will likely be disagreement on whether we go forward," he said. "In that decision there will be a level of risk and a level of certainty."

Decisions on other technologies likely will be even more subjective. For example, "if one wants to decide which software development technique is most appropriate for a particular set of the battle management software," reports the Eastport Study, "one can not make an objective assessment; it will likely rely at least partially on anecdotal evidence and the subjective judgement of experienced people."

More discussion is needed as to what exactly an early 1990s development decision will produce. Will it be a "go" or "no-go" decision on a baseline architecture with X number of phases and Y weapons that will take Z years to deploy? Or will it be a "go" or "no-go" decision on the general evolution of strategic defense with no precise projection of its dimensions or capabilities?

(4) There is a danger that schedule-driven research will force technological development to be reduced in order to achieve technology demonstrations for the early 1990s decision date. In other words, technological development and progress are frozen as SDI's research efforts and funds are diverted to build hardware that reflects the current state of technology. In this case, decision-makers would have their demonstration, but it would be at a lower technological level than if the demonstration deadline were extended until more sophisticated technology was available.

There already is evidence that reduction of technological research for demonstration projects is occurring. In order to avoid part of a $103 million cost overrun on AOA, the Airborne Optical

Adjunct (and no doubt its political fallout since the overrun surfaced just 8 months after the contract was awarded the to Boeing Company), SDI canceled a $62 million subcontract with Aerojet Electrosystems, which was to provide an advanced sensor for one of the two AOA planes to be demonstrated. The AOA plane would be deployed to track warheads in the late midcourse and early terminal phases of the defense.

SDI's handling of the cost overrun is disturbing. Aerojet was to develop a state-of-the-art sensor, which was to be more advanced than the sensor another subcontractor, Hughes Electro-optical and Data Systems Group, was to build using off-the-shelf technology. The Aerojet sensor was to have a different detection capability than the Hughes sensor—it was to be more sensitive, have a longer acquisition range, and be more resistant to nuclear effects.

In order to avoid a cost overrun and meet the same demonstration deadline, SDI dropped the Aerojet contract and will likely be demonstrating a less capable Hughes sensor on AOA. Not only that, but SDI has also forfeited the technology base Aerojet would have established with the development of its sensor. It also has lost the advantage of two types of sensor approaches, and has left itself in a risky position if the one AOA plane with the Hughes sensor experiences a catastrophic failure.

We questioned the overall value of AOA because of the limitations of passive discrimination. SDIO officials insist, however, that AOA is needed as a supplement to more sophisticated discrimination systems. If there is a supplemental role for AOA, and considering the severe technological hurdles AOA still must cross, particularly in a nuclear environment, the question arises as to whether the Aerojet contract should have been dropped and whether the demonstration deadline should have been temporarily left open-ended. As it now stands, decision-makers will get the demonstration, but it will be of a less capable system.

There is nothing unusual about military research programs having definable objectives and schedules for meeting them. There is also nothing disturbing about program managers striving to meet goals within a set schedule. The problem arises when the objectives are unrealistic and the deadlines are arbitrary. Congress, therefore, should ask two very important questions about the schedule-driven research SDI is pursuing:

First, what is the justification for an early 1990s development decision? Why is it so important to adhere to that deadline if it will entail risks? The authors of this study were offered no substantive justification for the early 1990s decision date. The Soviet ABM program was never cited as a reason. At this point, it appears to be an arbitrary date.

Second, what type of trade-off is there between adhering to an early 1990s development decision date and to extending the deadline to continue a vigorous research effort across a wide spectrum of technologies with the expectation of a more mature product? It is clear from the above discussion that an early 1990s decision carries adverse consequences, which must be weighed against the consequences of delaying that decision.

REORIENTATION TO NEAR-TERM DEPLOYMENT

After reviewing SDI's allocation of its FY1987 appropriation and the president's proposed SDI budget for FY1988, it is clear to us that another significant change has been taking place during 1987 in the SDI program. The SDI Organization originally envisioned that its research phase would last at least into the early 1990s and, depending on the funding, perhaps stretch into the mid-1990s. However, in response to pressure from within the administration and from some of SDI's more avid proponents in Congress, the SDI Organization has begun reorientating its program to deploy an initial token strategic defense system ahead of schedule, perhaps during 1994-1995. Our review of the FY 1987 and FY 1988 SDI budgets revealed the following evidence of efforts at an early deployment:

(1) The program's funding priority has been redirected from the directed energy weapons (DEW) budget to the kinetic energy weapons (KEW) budget. The DEW program is researching technologies for a far-term defense, while the KEW program has a heavy concentration of near-term technologies.

(2) In a number of instances, far-term innovative SDI technologies are being scaled back to pay for the near-term option.

(3) In the ground-based interceptor projects, SDI has cut back on the development of advanced technology while the early technology demonstrations of these interceptors is being heavily funded. The early demonstrations will not produce effective defense systems; only the far-term research will accomplish that. This appears to be an example of SDI being more interested in the near-term demonstration of a weapon than in taking the time necessary to develop an effective defensive system.

(4) SDI has scaled back research into space-based sensors that would be used for discrimination and tracking of warheads in the midcourse phase. Effective midcourse discrimination was always considered to be unavailable until near the end of the century.

(5) SDI has reorientated significantly its space-based kinetic kill vehicle (SBKKV) project to pursue a near-term deployment in the mid-1990s. Under orders from SDIO, the project is now pursuing an SBKKV system of much more limited capability than that previously considered essential for SDI boost-phase defensive systems.

(6) The SDI Organization, beginning in late 1986 and early 1987 conducted a highly classified study to draw-up a reference plan for a near-term deployment of strategic defenses.

While the political dimensions of the push for a near-term deployment is discussed in Chapter 5, it should be noted that this reorientation of strategic defenses has caused considerable turmoil within the SDI program. Basically, SDI scientists worry that the near-term push will greatly distort the program's priorities and the ultimate victim will be SDI research. In shifting to a near-term deployment, SDI in effect would be moving from a largely research program to predominantly an acquisitions program; that is, a program focused on erecting defenses rather than on researching which defense systems are the best. It is inevitable, according to one SDI scientist, that "major acquisitions will crowd out basic R&D funding."

Another SDI scientist explained: "If you want to deploy an initial operational capability by 1995 you have to lock in the technology you have now....If you go to engineering development now you can't expect to maintain a robust research program. There will be a big tendency to move ahead by 'eating your children.'" Not only is the far-term research inevitably reduced, the research in the immediate future becomes focused on resolving the problems at hand. "The near-term deployment will bias the research in that direction," declared another SDI scientist, adding that scientific efforts "will be devoted to resolving the critical issues involved with that deployment."

Another question raised in the weapons labs is whether, in fact, the scientific and engineering communities plus the defense contractors can work fast enough to achieve an early deployment in the 1994-1995 time frame. "There's a serious question of whether we can institutionally move to a 1994 initial operating capability," said one SDI scientist. "Unless there's a national emergency, it seems doubtful....We've built...this institutional slowness into military research. The administrative requirements alone add an extra year to any major research project." We might add that none of the SDI scientists we interviewed described any impending national emergency that would necessitate a crash program to deploy a strategic defense system in the near future.

TRANSPORTATION, SUPPORT & LOGISTICS

In considering the cost and complexity of a comprehensive strategic defense, both SDI proponents and opponents tend to focus on just the weapons, sensors, and battle management components that would be deployed. Indeed, these systems are daunting by themselves. The design studies envision hundreds of space-based platforms for the surveillance, tracking and acquisition of ICBMs and their warheads, thousands of space-based kinetic kill vehicle battle stations, a multitude of relay mirrors in space, battle management and C^3 satellites in geosynchronous orbit, hundreds of land-based radars and battle management centers, and tens of thousands of ground-based interceptor rockets.

Too often ignored, however, is the complex task of putting the strategic defense system in place and maintaining it. To get a idea of the cost and complexity of strategic defense one must superimpose over the system of weapons, sensors, and computers the substantial problems of transportation, support, and logistics (see Figure 9).

Figure 9

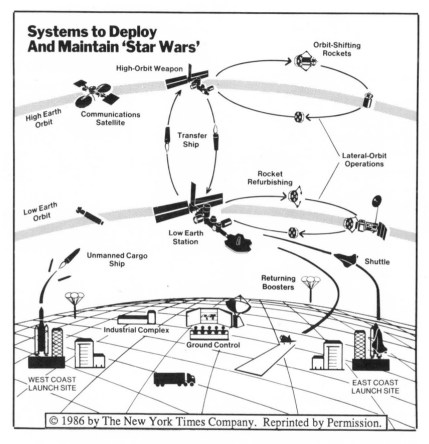

Systems to Deploy And Maintain 'Star Wars'

The minimal support needed to deploy and maintain a comprehensive strategic defense includes massive launch and recovery operations; an industrial complex to build the weapons and sensors, refurbishing operations for maintenance and conversions; mission control and planning operations; low-earth orbit and high-earth orbit operations to deploy and maintain space-based assets; inter-orbit operations and intra-orbit operations; communications operations to establish and maintain the nets; and an extensive ground transportation system. Indeed, the transportation and support system required for a comprehensive strategic defense may be as complex and unprecedented as the defense system itself.

So far, the debate over SDI has centered on whether the defense is feasible. However, serious questions should now be raised as to whether a transportation-support-logistics system for the defense is feasible.

SDI officials concede that the U.S. transportation-support-logistics system is currently inadequate and would entail too much cost to sustain a strategic defense. That is why General Abrahamson and other SDI officials are hesitant to estimate SDI deployment costs based on current U.S. capabilities. They prefer to base their estimates on what a strategic defense deployment *should* cost.

In order to make SDI affordable and cost-effective (one of Ambassador Nitze's criteria) there will have to be a substantial change in U.S. transportation-support-logistic capabilities. For this change to occur, SDI officials admit, there will have to be a revolution in the research, development, testing, and production methods of the Defense Department and the U.S. defense industry. What follows are but a few of the changes that must take place.

(1) *Henry Ford Production Techniques.* Presently, each U.S. satellite is individually handcrafted with no two exactly alike. More uniformity and efficiency is achieved with ground-based missiles and launchers, but not a great deal. Space shuttles cost about $2 billion each, MX missiles about $67 million each.

In order to make the tens of thousands of SDI missiles and satellites affordable, SDI officials say that assembly-line techniques (or "Henry Ford production methods") will have to be introduced. The aerospace and defense industry will have to undergo fundamental changes in their methods of production so that a missile will cost hundreds of thousands of dollars instead of millions, and a satellite will cost millions of dollars instead of hundreds of millions.

(2) *Transportation Requirements.* Presently, it costs $1,500 to $3,000 to put a pound of material into orbit. U.S. space shuttles and other launchers now place less than one million pounds into space per year. The Phase I design studies predicted that anywhere from 20 to 200 million pounds of SDI material will

have to be put in space. That will require 600 to 5,000 shuttle flights costing anywhere from $30 billion to $600 billion at current prices. SDI officials say the cost per pound will have to be reduced to between $200 and $400. See Figures 10 and 11 for the range of lift requirements. The basic requirements call for lifting 58 million pounds into orbit at a cost in current dollars of $87 billion to $174 billion for transportation alone.

Furthermore, the current space shuttle is too small for SDI's needs. Dr. William Lucas, former director of NASA's Marshall Space Flight Center, noted that 166 of the proposed SDIO payloads would not fit into shuttle craft's bay. Even before the loss of the Challenger, the shuttle was considered inadequate for SDI deployment, according to General Abrahamson's 1985 congressional testimony.

In the summer of 1985, Edward C. Aldridge, then Undersecretary of the Air Force, testified that NASA's and DoD's projected payloads through the 1990s would require between 19 and 24 space shuttle missions per year. This assumed four orbiters achieving 24 flights per year, no major problems with the shuttle, no commercial and foreign payloads in addition to NASA's payloads, no support for the Reagan-initiated space station, and no SDI deployments. A NASA official also testified that three space shuttle orbiters could sustain only 15 to 20 flights per year. Clearly, the loss of the Challenger, which leaves us with only three orbiters, presents a problem if the U.S. is to carry through with the Administration's space station initiative, develop SDI, maintain a vigorous military space program, and promote the commercialization of space. The administration's planned replacement for Challenger will still not be enough. It appears evident that other space transportation options will have to be developed.

To accomplish the launching of SDI space-based elements, a variety of heavy lift rockets and a hypersonic plane are under consideration. Current development schedules for heavy lift rockets indicate that Shuttle II, the successor to the current shuttle, will not be operational until after the year 2000. A single stage-to-orbit vehicle also will not be operational until about the year

2000. A derivative of the space shuttle that could launch materials into space at somewhat less expense than the current shuttle, although probably not cheap enough for SDIO's requirements, would not be operational until about 1995.

Figure 10

The Challenge

- 27 CANDIDATE ARCHITECTURES
  -- 20,000,000 to 200,000,000 lbs. to orbit
- IN PERSPECTIVE
  -- 600 to more than 5,000 space shuttle launches
- REPRESENTATIVE ARCHITECTURES DEVELOPED
  -- Representative at Architecture Level
  -- Realistic at System Level
  -- Baseline: 58,000,000 lbs. over 23-year period

Source: Department of Defense

The hypersonic plane under consideration has been variously called the National Aerospace Plane, the "X-plane," the trans-atmospheric vehicle (TAV), and, by President Reagan, the "Orient Express." Such a craft would be a revolutionary airbreathing airplane with engines capable of propelling it to 4,000 to 8,000 miles per hour in the upper atmosphere, then literally accelerating to sufficient speed to leave the atmosphere and achieve space orbit.

Figure 11

Current Costs

- SPACE SHUTTLE
  -- $100 To $180 Million Per Launch
  -- $100 Million Per Upper Stage
- COMPLEMENTARY EXPENDABLE LAUNCH VEHICLE
  -- $200 To $250 Million
- $1,500 TO $3,000/POUND
  -- $87 To $174 Billion To Launch Baseline Architecture

Source: Department of Defense

While George Keyworth, former White House Science Advisor, has claimed that the trans-atmospheric vehicle (TAV) could be available by the year 2000, NASA Associate Administrator Raymond Colladay called it "the most complex vehicle ever built" and SDIO's briefing chart did not envision it becoming operational until the year 2005—or about the time SDI presumably would have been deployed. While some see the TAV as a candidate launch vehicle for the strategic defense system, an SDI program manager was highly skeptical of its SDI potential, noting that for the moment the TAV has "more hype than possibility."

Even if a launch system is available for SDI at an affordable price, it would still require an enormous effort to get the space-based assets into orbit. SDI estimates that it could take as long as *eight years* to deploy the space defense system.

Setting aside the issue of which successor to the shuttle will be chosen, a critical question remains. What will it take to triple the current U.S. lift capacity and cut its cost almost tenfold in order to afford to place SDI into space?

"You would need a complete revolution in the way NASA operates," said one senior SDI official. "This is a national issue, not an SDI issue. The investment by this country into the cost effectiveness of launching vehicles in space has been essentially zero since the early '70s." To radically increase its launches and decrease its costs, NASA will "have to get rid of the manpower-intensive launch operation it now has," this official explained. Currently, 26,700 persons are engaged in space shuttle support. "We're going to have to get man out of the loop," he said, adding that he was not sure whether manned spaceflight will be required.

As huge as the space lift undertaking would be, SDIO in the past nevertheless has believed that a concerted effort to improve launch capacity could be put off until the monumental problems involved in producing strategic defense components were resolved. However, SDIO's attitude toward space transportation changed dramatically by 1987. Because of the near-term deployment push, SDI now appears to be pouring funds into its space transportation program.

When SDIO began reorientating its program towards early deployment, the biggest obstacle it faced was the absence of the space transportation required to lift thousands of SBKKV's into orbit. Moreover, no space transportation suitable for early deployment had been planned because no SDI demand for a low-cost, heavy-lift booster was anticipated before 1995. Furthermore, there was no other military or civilian space program that required such a booster. Early SDI deployment, however, required a new heavy-lift launch vehicle to haul the SBKKV hardware into space.

A heavy-lift launch vehicle is envisioned to put 100,000 to 150,000 pounds per launch into space, as compared with the space shuttle which lifts 20,000 to 50,000 pounds. SDI's original goal was to have, by the end of the century, a heavy-lift rocket that would reduce the cost of launching an object to orbit from the current $1,500 to $3,000 per pound to $200 to $400 per pound.

Air Force officials, however, now want to dramatically accelerate the heavy-lift program so that it could be operational by 1992 or 1993. That would mean design, development, testing, and flight certification of a space transportation system in about five years. Such an acceleration of the original heavy-lift program would be impossible to accomplish if the Air Force also wanted to meet SDI's original cost reduction goal. Air Force and SDI officials, therefore, have told their rocket engineers to take the design they envisioned for a turn-of-the-century, heavy-lift rocket and work backwards to determine what could be done for a near-term, heavy-lift rocket.

As a result, SDI now is seeking as a *goal* a near-term, heavy-lift vehicle which, instead of lifting material into space for $200 to $400 per pound, will launch hardware at a cost of $1,000 per pound. The Air Force Systems Command, in fact, has formally told contractors it wants a heavy-lift vehicle (or an advanced launch system, as the Air Force now terms it) that lifts material into space at substantially reduced costs by 1993 or 1994 and a subsequent vehicle by 1998 that reduces launch costs by an order of magnitude.

(3) *Support Activities.* A number of auxiliary activities in support of SDI will have to undergo fundamental changes. For example, the Fletcher Panel implied that SDI's communication network would be based on the defense system's own basic units. The Eastport Study believes, however, that a separate network of communications satellites is needed to support the defense system. If so, that will necessitate change. "The existing communications

technology cannot support the special requirements of the envisioned strategic defense system," the Eastport Study concluded, adding that existing communications security systems also "are not suitable for strategic defense."

HURDLES CONFRONTING INNOVATION

Of particular concern to the Eastport Study was the fact that many technology innovations never survive the Pentagon bureaucracy. As a result, defense technology often lags behind state-of-the-art technology. SDI will have to break this pattern so that research can be conducted in innovative technologies and so that more affordable weapons systems can be produced.

As the Eastport Study noted:

> It will be necessary to propagate a different culture of system development that will exploit the emerging technologies....The endless demands of project schedules, the lack of capable staff, the lack of capital equipment, the 'not-invented-here' syndrome, the conservatism in procurement decisions, and bureaucracy have created a new culture that resists change and takes only naive risks. SDIO must create a new culture that can adapt to changes more effectively.

In other words, SDI cannot become just another weapons program fraught with delays, cost overruns, and bureaucratic inertia. To be affordable, it must break that mold.

Can the Department of Defense and the U.S. defense industry undergo this revolution to attain the production efficiencies needed to make SDI affordable? Can a more economical system be devised to deploy and maintain a strategic defense system? Can military research, development and procurement practices be changed to produce complex weapons systems less expensively than previously imagined? Can the space industry be catapulted into a more efficient and vastly expanded form of operation? Can decades of entrenched administrative behavior in the Pentagon, aerospace and defense industries, and NASA be radically altered?

SDI officials remain remarkably sanguine about the revolution that must occur. They believe there can be change, particularly as a new generation of researchers, engineers, and military leaders are introduced to the new requirements of strategic defense. Congress, however, should be wary of optimistic assessments. If the past is any guide, administrative and sociological hurdles are as difficult to overcome as the technological ones.

ADMINISTRATION

We were impressed with SDI's officials, managers, scientists and engineers. From General Abrahamson on down, they displayed an unusually high degree of professionalism and dedication to the mission they have been assigned. Nevertheless, some problems are surfacing in SDI management and administration.

There is some duplication of services among the laboratories and the military agencies working on SDI research. For example, both the Army and the Air Force have their own systems, battle management, and support offices. For the moment, it is open to question whether this duplication is harmful or helpful. In the future, they will have to be consolidated for greater efficiency and effectiveness.

Service rivalry, particularly between the Army and the Air Force, is creeping into the SDI program and it is likely to get worse before it gets better. There also appears to be some tension growing among the SDI organization, the services, and the laboratories. This tension could be exacerbated by large increases in SDI's funding, which the services and labs complain are resulting in less, and in some cases inadequate, funding for other vital military research.

There also is a growing rivalry among the national laboratories researching SDI. In some respects this rivalry can be healthy. However, it can be detrimental, SDI scientists warn, when it leads to labs making unsubstantiated claims of success for their own work or unfair criticisms of the work of other labs. For example, some SDI scientists were deeply concerned over high officials at the Livermore Laboratory issuing inflated claims about the X-ray laser's capabilities. Scientists, including some at Livermore, also believe that inflated claims by lab and SDI officials of the research's progress could adversely affect the credibility of the laboratories.

Chapter 4

SDI and Arms Control

Any examination of SDI must consider the Anti-Ballistic Missile (ABM) Treaty of 1972 because of the limitations the treaty imposes on the strategic defense program. The treaty prohibits national or regional ballistic missile defenses; additionally, it forbids the development, testing, or deployment of any space-based ABM system or component. The U.S.-U.S.S.R. summit in Iceland suggests that future arms control negotiations between the superpowers will inevitably focus on SDI and expand or contract the treaty-imposed restrictions on the SDI program.

THE ABM TREATY

This is not a minor treaty. It is the cornerstone of our arms control agreements, the only permanent bilateral arms control accord between the United States and the Soviet Union.

President Reagan urged Americans to envision an SDI peace shield over the United States. He did not mention, however, that any deployment or even *development* decision for SDI would require the U.S. to withdraw from, abandon, or modify the ABM Treaty. When the President did mention the ABM Treaty he assured Americans that in conducting SDI *research,* the U.S. would abide by the treaty. That SDI lies on a collision course with the ABM Treaty was left unstated.

BACKGROUND OF THE TREATY

By 1965, the U.S.S.R. was deploying a ballistic missile defense system after researching BMD since the early 1950s. Initially, the Soviets rejected U.S. overtures to limit BMD systems, but by 1969 they indicated a willingness to pursue such a limitation. Negotiations proceeded for two and a half years and culminated in a treaty in May 1972.

The Soviets evidently realized that their technology was inadequate for a nationwide defense, especially against U.S. ICBMs carrying multiple warheads, and would be extraordinarily costly to deploy.   The U.S. had perhaps a 10-year BMD research lead over the Soviets, but ultimately decided even its technology was not cost-effective against the growing Soviet threat.

Since the 1950s, the U.S. has worked on a variety of ABM systems including an early 1960s boost-phase rocket defense program called Project BAMBI (ballistic missile boost intercept). However, every President since Truman had decided against a nationwide BMD deployment. Robert McNamara, Secretary of Defense for President Johnson, proposed deployment of a "thin" ABM defense against a Chinese attack on our population. On taking office, President Nixon called for review of the McNamara proposal and ultimately rejected it. Deciding defense of our missile deterrent force was more feasible than population defense, Nixon proposed an ABM defense of Minuteman silos at Grand Forks, North Dakota. Ultimately, even that project was canceled because of its enormous cost and dubious military utility.

WHAT'S IN THE TREATY

The preamble to the treaty (see Appendix B) states, "...effective measures to limit BMD systems would be a substantial factor in curbing the race in strategic offensive arms and would lead to a decrease in the risk of outbreak of war involving nuclear weapons." It also says, "the limitation of antiballistic missile systems...would contribute to the creation of more favorable conditions for further negotiations on limiting strategic arms."   The Reagan administration apparently rejects both premises, believing SDI will curb the arms race by making nuclear weapons impotent and obsolete, and thus refuses to negotiate significant limitations on SDI.

The treaty contains a series of prohibited activities. With one exception no ABM system may defend the territory of the nation, nor any region of the nation. The exception is that under Article III a very limited, fixed (nonmobile), land-based ABM system may be deployed at Grand Forks, North Dakota, and around Moscow. The deployment of ABM systems or even their components, except for the very limited Article III systems, is prohibited by the treaty. Neither country may develop, test, or deploy ABM systems or components which are sea-based, air-based, space-based, or mobile land-based (Article V). Giving missiles or radars (such as in air-defenses) an ABM capability to counter strategic ballistic missiles in flight trajectory is prohibited (Article VI[a]). Deployment of radars capable of directing BMD systems is prohibited. The only exception to this prohibition is radars deployed along the periphery of a country for early warning of a strategic nuclear attack. Transfer of prohibited ABM systems or components to other countries is prohibited as is deployment of ABM systems or components outside the national territory (Article IX). Article II defines an ABM system as one "to counter strategic ballistic missiles or their elements in flight." Therefore, the treaty would not cover an anti-tactical ballistic missile system.

In addition to the treaty's prohibitions are several permissible activities. As noted above, Article III permits one ABM system around Moscow and one system at Grand Forks, North Dakota, each with no more than 100 ABM launchers and limited ABM radars. Originally the Treaty permitted a choice of defending either the nation's capitol or an ICBM silo field; but under a 1974 protocol (see Appendix B) the U.S. elected to protect the missiles at Grand Forks and the U.S.S.R. elected to protect Moscow. The treaty permits modernization and replacement of the Article III ABM systems and their components. To develop and test systems for Grand Forks and Moscow, each nation may also have 15 ABM launchers at agreed test ranges.

Although the treaty is of unlimited duration, either party may give 6 months notice to withdraw from the accord if it decides "extraordinary events related to the subject matter of this Treaty have jeopardized its supreme interests" (Article XV). The parties also agreed to establish a Standing Consultative Commission to discuss questions arising under the treaty.

SDI AND THE ABM TREATY

Article I of the treaty provides that: "Each Party undertakes not to deploy ABM systems for a defense of the territory of its country...." It also prohibits ABM deployment to defend even a region of the nation, save for the limited deployments at Grand Forks, North Dakota and Moscow. Therefore deployment of any ABM system, other than at Grand Forks, capable of defending the entire population of the U.S. is inconsistent with the treaty. Deployment of an SDI system based in space is inconsistent with the treaty, not only because of its purported capability (nationwide defense) but also because Article V of the treaty prohibits development, testing or deployment of ABM systems or components that are "sea-based, air-based, space-based, or mobile land-based."

The treaty's prohibition on ABM deployment would not immediately constrain SDI because its deployment is not likely to occur until at least the mid-1990s. The treaty's prohibition on development and testing of ABM systems, however, could be soon breached by the United States. The SDI program's desire for a full-scale engineering development decision early in the 1990s requires the development or testing of a space-based SDI system or components which would be inconsistent with the ABM treaty. The same goes for ABM systems aboard aircraft or at sea.

The treaty does not explicitly define the term "develop" but its meaning was discussed during the negotiations. Senator Henry M. Jackson queried Ambassador Gerard C. Smith, chief negotiator of the ABM Treaty, on this point before the Senate Armed Services Committee. Smith responded that:

The obligation not to develop such systems, devices, or warheads would be applicable only to that stage of development which follows laboratory development and testing. The prohibitions on development contained in the ABM Treaty would start at that part of the development process where field testing is initiated on either a prototype or breadboard model. It was understood by both sides that the prohibition of "development action" applies to activities involved after a component moves from the laboratory development and testing stage to the field testing stage, wherever performed. The fact that early stages of the development process, such as laboratory testing, would pose problems for verification by national technical means is an important consideration in reaching this definition. Exchanges with the Soviet Delegation made clear that this definition is also the Soviet interpretation of the term "development." ...Article V...places no constraints on research and on those aspects of exploratory and advanced development which precede field testing. Engineering development would clearly be prohibited. Nevertheless, this was never reduced to an Agreed Statement among the parties.

Whereas the treaty forbids deployment, testing, and development of space-based ABM systems or their components, it does not forbid ABM "research." In fact, the term "research" is never used in the treaty. There is general agreement that, by implication, ABM research is permitted. The issue is at what point does research become development or testing.

The treaty's prohibitions refer to "ABM systems or their components." Article II lists the components of an ABM system as being interceptor missiles, launchers, and radars. But for exotic technologies, such as lasers, there may be no direct analog for these components. Arguably, these prohibitions do not apply to ABM *subcomponents*, system "adjuncts," or other elements of an ABM system that are less than components. In planning its SDI experiments, the administration has pledged to abide by the treaty, but it is making full use of distinctions between components and lesser elements. The problem is that if these distinctions are exploited by the U.S. or the U.S.S.R. beyond the ability of either side to independently verify compliance, then the claim of compliance will soon ring hollow for both sides.

Most observers think the SDI research program will not present serious compliance questions until 1988. However, General Abrahamson has admitted that by the turn of the decade, the SDI program will require us "to depart from the treaty." The briefings and interviews conducted for our initial report revealed that a premature U.S. termination of the ABM treaty and the SALT accords could have adverse consequences not only for U.S. national security but also the SDI program.

Some of SDI's supporters have maintained that the ABM Treaty is no longer in the U.S. national security interest and is holding back SDI research. The authors could find no credible evidence of SDI research at this early stage being adversely affected by the ABM Treaty. No doubt early SDI tests and experiments could be conducted that would violate the ABM treaty. The case has not been made, however, that these experiments would be necessary at this point for the overall progress of the research.

On the contrary, a violation at this point could do serious harm to U.S. security and the SDI program. As one senior officer deeply involved in SDI research admitted, "It is not in our interest to violate the ABM Treaty at this point because of the Soviet breakout capability."

There is also the belief among some SDI proponents that the current U.S.-Soviet strategic arms limitation agreements, particularly SALT II, are not in our national security interests. SDI officials, however, claim that the SALT limits are presently in their best interest. "I would not like to see the Soviets go beyond the SALT limits," said General Abrahamson. The reason is simple. A U.S.-Soviet breakout of SALT only compounds the problems SDI faces in both the near and far term. It could mean a doubling of the Soviet strategic warheads within a decade; by the end of the century, the number of their RVs might be quadrupled.

REINTERPRETING THE TREATY

Since the ABM treaty's ratification every administration, including initially the Reagan administration, has interpreted it generally along the lines described above. Indeed, the Reagan administration's 1985 Arms Control Impact Statement submitted to Congress stated:

The ABM Treaty prohibition on development, testing and deployment of space-based ABM systems or components for such systems applies to directed energy technology or any other technology used for this purpose.

On October 2, 1985, the 13th anniversary of the accord becoming effective, a proposed summit with the Soviet Union was only 6 weeks away and the ABM treaty was a likely topic for discussion. On that anniversary, six former secretaries of defense jointly called on the U.S. and the U.S.S.R. to "avoid actions that would undermine the ABM Treaty." Having served five presidents over 18 years, former secretaries Harold Brown, Clark Clifford, Melvin Laird, Robert McNamara, Elliott Richardson, and James Schlesinger urged President Reagan and General Secretary Gorbachev to agree to negotiate new measures to prevent further erosion of the treaty and to assure its continued viability. Specifically mentioned as an element of that erosion was the Soviet radar installation at Krasnoyarsk in Siberia, which appears to violate Article VI of the treaty because it is not on the periphery of the national territory and oriented outward.

But unexpectedly, on October 6, 1985, Robert McFarlane, then national security advisor to the president, casually asserted on the nationally televised program "Meet the Press" that the ABM treaty permitted the development and testing of those ABM systems that are based on exotic technologies; that is, on new physical concepts not available to ABM systems when the document was signed. In other words, the development and testing of SDI "exotic" technologies would not clash with the ABM treaty. This unilateral reinterpretation of the ABM treaty was a bombshell, but two days later the White House confirmed it to be administration policy.

From where had this reinterpretation arisen? On April 4, 1985, the Heritage Foundation issued a paper arguing that the treaty does not restrict development *or even deployment* of SDI. The author of the paper was "a scholar, currently employed in the Administration, who requests anonymity."

On July 25, 1985, Senator Carl Levin of the Senate Armed Services Committee asked the Department of Defense to answer questions about the precise definition of some of the terms in the

ABM treaty. Subsequently, in early September 1985, Fred C. Ikle, Undersecretary of Defense for Policy, and Richard Perle, Assistant Defense Secretary for International Security Policy, hired a former assistant district attorney with no prior arms control experience to review the treaty and the secret negotiating records to determine its effect on SDI. By mid-September, the attorney produced a 19-page report reinterpreting the treaty to permit SDI development and testing.

Richard Perle presented these revelations to an administration interagency committee. Secretary of State George Schultz requested the State Department's legal adviser to examine the issue. That adviser, Abraham Sofaer, wrote a series of memorandums concluding that the treaty does *not* ban testing or development of ABM systems based on exotic technology, but that deployment was barred.

On October 4, the Special Arms Control Policy Group, chaired by McFarlane, met at the White House to discuss the reinterpretation, but no formal agreement was reached among the officials. Two days later, McFarlane unexpectedly announced that testing and development of ABM systems based on new physical concepts are "approved and authorized by the treaty."

The uproar that resulted over the reinterpretation (particularly among U.S. allies) apparently led Schultz to appeal to the president on October 11 to reject it. The president decided that the administration would adopt the "broad interpretation" as the correct legal interpretation, but that the SDI research program would for the time being comply with the traditional or "strict" interpretation of the treaty. The 1986 Report to Congress on the Strategic Defense Initiative said "the Administration applies the more restrictive treaty interpretation as a matter of policy, although we are not legally required to do so, in evaluating the experiments in the SDI program." Simultaneously, the administration reserved "the right to conduct the SDI program under the broad interpretation at some future time."

The consultation involved in the administration's decision to reinterpret the treaty was minimal. Later congressional hearings revealed that none of the European allies was consulted prior to

October 6. The Soviet Union was not consulted, although the treaty specifically provides for a Standing Consultative Commission to "consider questions concerning compliance with the obligations assumed and related situations which may be considered ambiguous."

Consultation with the treaty's 1972 negotiating team would have seemed prudent before reinterpreting the treaty. No one on the team was consulted except Paul Nitze. He later conceded that his recollection of the treaty's meaning did not agree with the reinterpretation view. Since seeing the new interpretation, however, he has now adopted it and believes it is the correct view.

The reinterpretation holds that during the ABM Treaty negotiations, the U.S. tried *but failed* to get the Soviets to agree to limit the *development* and *testing of future* ABM systems based on "exotic technologies." Therefore, the treaty does not prohibit development and testing of exotic systems such as those employing laser weapons.

What is the basis for this assertion? Article V of the treaty seems clear enough: "Each Party undertakes not to develop, test, or deploy ABM systems or components which are sea-based, air-based, space-based or mobile land-based." However, reinterpretation advocates say one must look at the treaty's definition of "ABM systems."

Article II defines them as "a system to counter strategic ballistic missiles or their elements in flight trajectory, currently consisting of...ABM interceptor missiles,...ABM launchers, ...ABM radars...." Those advocating reinterpretation allege this means ABM systems that do not consist of these elements are not covered as ABM systems under the treaty. The traditional view is that the use of the words "currently consisting of," the preceding comma, and the terms that follow are merely illustrative and do not comprise a list of requisite elements of a covered ABM system.

The most critical element in the reinterpretation case is Agreed Statement D, which is not in the text of the treaty. This list of Agreed Statements was signed by the heads of the delegations on the same day the treaty was signed.

Reinterpretation proponents argue that Agreed Statement D implies that ABM systems based "on other physical principles" are only subject to future discussion and amendments under the treaty. Thus, Statement D and the definition of "ABM system" in Article II, read together, exempt exotic ABM systems altogether from the Article V prohibitions on development and testing.

Ambassador Smith flatly rejected the reinterpretation's validity, insisting it would "make a dead letter" of the ABM Treaty. John Rhinelander, former legal advisor to the ABM negotiations, argued that the rationale for the broad interpretation "...is absurd as a matter of policy, intent, and interpretation."

CONSEQUENCES OF THE REINTERPRETATION

As SDI is still in the research phase, no one knows if a viable, cost-effective system will ever emerge from it. The administration claims SDI research will be governed for now by the restrictive interpretation of the treaty. Therefore, announcing the reinterpretation apparently gained us nothing, but left us no room to object if the Soviets decide to abide by no more than our "reinterpretation" of the treaty.

The administration complains that the stumbling block to an arms control agreement is Soviet insistence on bilateral treaty amendments to restrict SDI. Yet, we *unilaterally* reinterpreted the treaty to eliminate any legal restrictions on the development or testing of "exotic" ABM systems. Our pledge to remain within the strict interpretation is undercut by our reserving the right to abide by the reinterpretation at the president's discretion. This has done nothing to enhance the reputation of our nation as one that stands by its treaties.

Ambassador Paul Nitze, special advisor to the president and the secretary of state on arms control matters, testified that the controversy over reinterpretation is "moot" because SDI research will comply with the strict interpretation anyway. However, the point is hardly moot because the American negotiating position on arms control at Reykjavik was based on the reinterpretation.

ICELAND SUMMIT

The meeting on October 10-12, 1986, between President Reagan and Secretary General Gorbachev in Reykjavik, Iceland, was billed as only a "preparatory summit" between the two leaders to set the date and agenda for the real summit in Geneva, the first such U.S.-Soviet meeting in six years. U.S. spokesmen emphasized that the preliminary meeting had modest objectives, and they sought to prevent expectations from soaring. Admiral John Poindexter, who had replaced McFarlane as national security adviser, told the press after the meeting, "we thought the best that we could probably hope to get out of Iceland was a focusing of the agenda for a Washington summit."

The Soviet objective, however, was to focus attention on arms control as the agenda and, in particular, on SDI. Why were the Soviets apparently worried about SDI? Why do they continue to be worried? While some individuals point to Soviet concern over SDI as justification enough for the program, further scrutiny of Soviet concerns is warranted.

First, the Soviets claim that SDI is a U.S. effort to achieve strategic superiority by acquiring a first-strike capability. They argue that, with an effective defense shield in place, the U.S. could launch a first-strike attack on the Soviet Union and then use its strategic defenses to parry any retaliatory blow. It is interesting, but no doubt a coincidence, that the Soviets in discussing SDI refer to it as "space strike arms." As early as 1965, Phyllis Schlafly and General Chester Charles Ward argued in *Strike From Space* for U.S. deployment of space-based, boost-phase defenses, and other space weapons to achieve military superiority over the Soviet Union. Even President Reagan concedes that our unilaterally combining offensive and defensive strategic weapons could be perceived by the Soviets as seeking a first-strike capability. That is why he proposes giving the Soviets the benefits of SDI technology and mutually eliminating offensive missiles, followed by our mutual deployment of strategic defenses. The Soviets are suspicious of our offer to share SDI technology. Gorbachev noted dryly after Reykjavik that the U.S. currently limits the sale of dairy technology to the Soviet Union.

Second, the Soviets claim that SDI will inevitably lead to an arms race in space, a realm that is, as yet, not fully militarized. They seem unconvinced that transition to strategic defenses can be stabilizing and controlled.

Third, the Soviets claim that there can be no arms control agreement limiting strategic offensive arms unless the U.S. agrees to Soviet demands for limitations on SDI research. The Soviets have suggested that their chief countermeasure to SDI will be proliferation of their offensive weapons. Thus, they cannot accept limitations at the bargaining table on their offensive arms unless the U.S. agrees to ironclad limitations on SDI.

Finally, there are other reasons, besides those they acknowledge, why the Soviets might fear SDI. Matching our efforts in SDI will necessitate head-to-head competition in computers, guidance systems, sensors and space technology—areas where the U.S. lead is substantial. Even if SDI proves feasible, the Soviets might not want to enter a race that emphasizes our strengths and their weaknesses.

Moreover, the Soviets might fear that SDI will undermine their economic plans. Gorbachev has launched a very ambitious program for economic revitalization of the Soviet economy. If he is serious about this revitalization, the cost of deploying strategic defenses in space could severely limit these plans.

Finally, vehement Soviet opposition to SDI could be a propaganda ploy. They might see SDI as a means of depicting themselves to the world as proponents of arms control and the U.S. pursuit of SDI as the chief obstacle to an arms agreement. Their short-lived advocacy of "Star Peace," Gorbachev's recent declarations about the immorality of the arms race, and his rhetoric after Reykjavik suggest the possibility of such a ploy.

Much has been made of SDI's value as a bargaining chip in the arms talks. Several proponents claim that SDI alone brought the Soviets back to the bargaining table, although Ambassador Nitze on April 29, 1989, called this an "oversimplification" and said that

SDI "played a part" along with other important factors in the Soviet decision to return.

SDI advocates repeatedly have asserted on Capitol Hill that failure to fund SDI at the requested budget levels would undermine U.S. negotiating leverage at Geneva. SDI critics have countered that—because administration officials insist that SDI research is non-negotiable at the arms talks—the funding level for the research program is of little consequence to our negotiating position. Ultimately, it has become clear that SDI will have no value as a bargaining chip unless it is played. At Iceland, President Reagan proved unwilling to play the chip.

The Russians by 1985 had already outlined their arms control proposal for reducing nuclear arms and limiting SDI. In short, SDI would be restricted to laboratory research; deliverable strategic nuclear warheads would be reduced by approximately 50% to 6,000 for each side; development of new offensive strategic nuclear weapons systems, such as Midgetman and Trident II, would be banned.

President Reagan had outlined his so-called "5-2-6" strategic arms offer in a letter to Secretary Gorbachev in July 1986. Under that offer both sides would agree to confine themselves for five years to research, development, and testing of strategic defenses (which the president argued was permitted by the ABM treaty) to determine whether advanced systems of strategic defense are technically feasible. Thereafter if either side decided to deploy an ABM system, they must offer to negotiate within two years a plan for sharing the benefits of strategic defense and for eliminating offensive ballistic missiles. If no such agreement is reached in two years, then either side could deploy its ABM system after giving 6 months notice.

This notion of sharing SDI technology and eliminating all offensive missiles was not new to President Reagan. In his speech of March 23, 1983, initiating SDI, he declared that: "I clearly recognize that defense systems have limitations and raise certain problems and ambiguities. If paired with offensive systems, they can be viewed as fostering an aggressive policy and no one wants that."

Thus, in his first SDI speech Reagan conceded that the combination of defensive ABM systems and offensive missiles could be perceived as threatening to the opposing side. Thereafter, he sought ways to neutralize this destabilizing aspect of SDI. On October 21, 1984, Reagan offered to *give* our SDI technology to the Soviets once it had proven effective. Surely this would calm Soviet fears as to our intentions with regard to SDI. Again, on October 25, 1985, he offered to *share* SDI technology with the Soviets. On October 31, 1985, he went a step further, pledging not to deploy SDI until we did away with our offensive nuclear missiles. The press wondered if this didn't give the Soviets, in effect, a veto over SDI because we surely would not abandon our offensive missiles until the Soviets did likewise.

President Reagan responded on November 6, 1985, claiming he had been misunderstood. If the Soviets did not agree to eliminate nuclear weapons, "we would go ahead with deployment" of SDI. However, he returned to his original concern by adding:

> But even though, as I say, that would then open us to the charge of achieving the capacity for a first strike. We don't want that. We want to eliminate things of that kind.

Well before Reykjavik, Reagan recognized that SDI could be perceived as destabilizing as long as we possessed offensive missiles. If, he reasoned, we shared the benefits of SDI technology with the Soviets to enable both sides to build missile defenses and we agreed to a mutual ban on offensive nuclear missiles, then SDI would shed the provocative or aggressive aura attributed to it.

In Iceland, the Soviets lost no time in laying out a comprehensive arms control proposal. After intense negotiation on October 11 and the morning of October 12, tentative agreement was reached on the elements of a broad compromise, except for strategic defense.

How far apart were they? A tentative agreement was reached to eliminate INF (intermediate range nuclear forces) in Europe and maintain 100 INF warheads worldwide on each side. On strategic offensive arms, a general framework of an agreement emerged to reduce strategic warheads by 50% in five years and then in the following five years (a total of 10 years) to eliminate all ballistic missiles (a U.S. proposal) or all strategic nuclear weapons (a U.S.S.R. proposal).

The Soviets, however, tied agreement on any item to settlement of SDI issues. Here the two superpowers' positions appeared to be far apart. The heart of their differences was the ABM treaty. The Soviets wanted the duration of the treaty to remain infinite. The U.S. wanted to abolish it in 10 years and to permit general deployment of ABM systems. Although the two sides agreed to abide by the treaty during the interim period, each side had a different treaty in mind.

President Reagan told Americans on October 14, 1986 that at Reykjavik the U.S. offered to "proceed with research, development and testing of SDI–all done in conformity with ABM provisions." What he did not mention was that the U.S. agreed to be bound, not by the traditional, strict interpretation, but by the administration's reinterpretation of the ABM treaty. This was unambiguously confirmed by Admiral Poindexter on October 13, 1986, when a reporter pressed him. Thus, under the U.S. offer research, development, and testing of exotic SDI technologies could proceed unincumbered for the 10-year period.

The Soviets insisted on strict adherence to the traditional interpretation of the ABM treaty and, in fact, insisted on "strengthening" the treaty to say, "Testing of all space elements of antiballistic defense in space is prohibited except research and testing in laboratories." Some U.S. observers believe the Soviets yet may be flexible on this language.

Reykjavik added yet another interesting dimension to SDI. The current research program presumes that a deployed system would face a massive Soviet arsenal of thousands of warheads and tens of thousands of decoys. Under President Reagan's suggestion that SDI might be an "insurance policy" after the elimination of all ballistic missiles, the defensive system would face at most a few clandestine missiles, a much more manageable problem for the defense.

However, as the task becomes manageable the need for a deployed system becomes questionable. On this point, Henry Kissinger in the *Washington Post* on November 18, 1986 asked:

...if the U.S. can do without strategic defense in the 10 years when, under the American scheme, ballistic missiles are retained, why is it necessary to acquire a missile defense after ballistic missiles are eliminated? At that point a defense against airplanes would make much more sense.

Chapter 5

Politics and SDI

From its inception, SDI has had all the appearances of a politically inspired program. It was announced with little prior notification of or consultation with relevant Defense and State Department experts. Stories of all kinds flew about Washington for months after the President's March 1983 announcement. One had it that a high ranking Defense Department official responsible for developing strategic policy, when notified by phone of the President's 1983 speech, expressed concern that the President's vision of a world dominated by strategic defense seemed like a futuristic cartoon. As evidence of the political power of the "Star Wars" concept, however, this same official is now one of the program's most outspoken supporters.

It is fair to question how an idea with so little prior scientific review could garner so much support. Like all good political programs SDI offered something for everybody.

First, during the 1980s the American public had become more aware of the danger of a nuclear holocaust. The causes and consequences of such a catastrophe had been the subject of numerous television documentaries, such as *Nuclear Winter* and *Facing up to the Bomb*, and television theater, such as *The Day After*. More important politically, the nuclear freeze movement had entered actively into the congressional campaign of 1982 with an alternative to nuclear war—a demand for the Reagan administration to take the initiative in negotiations with the U.S.S.R. to halt the nuclear arms race.

That the U.S.'s official strategic policy had evolved from the idea of "massive retaliation" in the 1950s to the more restrictive targeting concept of "flexible response" in the 1980s was lost on most Americans who saw any use of nuclear weapons as inevitably resulting in catastrophic destruction. To many of these Americans, Reagan's SDI proposal offered hope that U.S. space-based lasers might neutralize hostile nuclear weapons. No doubt these hopes were reinforced by TV's animated explanations of SDI where life-like images of lasers unerringly zapped Soviet missiles.

Second, SDI feeds the persistent, if somewhat shaken, American belief that Yankee inventiveness and industrial ingenuity can find a technological answer to the threat posed by Soviet nuclear-tipped ICBMs. Americans want to believe that their technological superiority, so evident during the past century, is capable of meeting this new challenge. Moreover, reliance on a policy of mutual deterrence does not square with America's traditional desire to go-it-alone abroad. Why must U.S. survival depend on Soviet nuclear restraint if it is within our power to regain control of our national future and security?

Third, SDI's possible technological solution to America's defensive needs was enthusiastically endorsed by those Americans who dislike the prospect of political dealings with the "evil empire," the Soviet Union. These hard-liners frequently had chastised earlier administrations for negotiating arms control and other agreements with the U.S.S.R., believing that such undertakings reduced America's ability to defend itself and encouraged Soviet ambitions. A successful SDI program would mean that future arms control negotiations with Moscow would be conducted on the U.S.'s terms or not at all. Therefore, who needs a treaty which depends on mutual forbearance and verification if instead lasers could do the job?

Finally, in addition to a grand goal and a futuristic vision, SDI offers lucrative contracts to a defense and aerospace industry besieged by Defense Department auditors, congressional critics, the press, and foreign competitors. SDI also fills a vacuum left by administrations that have been ambivalent or inconsistent in their support for strategic nuclear weapons and for such civilian programs as NASA, the space station, and space exploration.

The political right and left have reacted strongly to SDI. The right (including President Reagan) has made support for SDI a test of patriotism and administration loyalty. Otherwise moderate politicians have found it difficult to express reasonable doubts about the program, or to even ask pertinent questions, without incurring the wrath of the right and the administration. The left immediately rejected SDI and set out to stop the program. While examination of their views is beyond the scope of this study, it may be noted that they objected to SDI because: (a) it was technically unworkable; (b) it ignored facing up to the political realities of U.S.-Soviet relations; and (c) it would stimulate a new arms race and, thereby, create an even more threatening nuclear world. (The bibliography contains references to these and other arguments.)

Before examining the congressional debate over SDI and its funding during the past two years, it is helpful to consider the context in which this debate occurred.

BUDGETARY CONSTRAINTS AND SDI

The 99th Congress (1985-86) in the waning hours of 1985 passed a watershed piece of legislation. Formally known as the Balanced Budget and Emergency Deficit Control Act of 1985, the Gramm-Rudman-Hollings legislation required Congress to balance the Federal budget over a five-year period ending in FY 1992 by reducing spending $36 billion per year. Its authors were Senator Phil Gramm (R-Tex.), Senator Warren Rudman (R-N.H.), and Senator Ernest Hollings (D-S.C.).

That the Congress, which had summarily rejected other budget balancing amendments as superficial and inadequate, chose to pass the Gramm-Rudman-Hollings legislation appears to be more an indication of frustration on Capitol Hill than of the efficacy of this particular scheme. Many senators and representatives were frustrated because Congress could not come to grips with the deficit by altering spending patterns. The Gramm-Rudman-Hollings legislation was also an expression of deep congressional frustration with a president, who having received a forty-nine-state electoral mandate a short year before, refused to work with legislators on the most difficult issues of governing.

In January 1986, while court challenges threatened the constitutionality of the Gramm-Rudman-Hollings act, the talk in Washington was of a possible fall "sequester." This term, which had been more recently reserved for juries, was being restored to its original Latin meaning of seizing property—in this case government spending programs. Under the Gramm-Rudman-Hollings law, if Congress and the president were unable to reach an agreement that would meet the deficit targets in a given year, a "sequestration" order would be instituted by the Office of Management and Budget and the Congressional Budget Office and supervised by the General Accounting Office. The order would require an across-the-board percentage reduction of nearly every item in the federal budget in order to reach the prescribed targets.

As part of the legislative agreement on the original Gramm-Rudman-Hollings legislation, Congress approved an initial sequester for FY 1986 of $11.7 billion to be divided equally between defense and domestic programs. The sequester was adopted in order to demonstrate that Congress could summon the resolve to impose spending cuts; however, the reduction was modest to avoid chaos in the budget. The administration was given limited discretion to protect what it deemed to be high priority programs. Predictably, one of the programs the White House chose to protect was SDI.

This move had a number of ramifications. The protection given SDI signaled to Congress that its previous support of the program was not given without a price. Every weapons program and military research project took a share of the across-the-board Gramm-Rudman-Hollings reductions, that is, every program save the SDI. Moreover, because SDI happens to be situated among the Defense Agencies research and development accounts, the other Defense Agencies programs received double the percentage reduction in order to offset SDI's exemption.

Next, SDI's protected status told the military that its conventional priorities took a backseat to Star Wars. Budget allocations for tanks, ships, and airplanes were all cut. Even though some of these items were being produced at limited, uneconomic production rates before the cuts, they were not spared. In addition, SDI's protected status signaled to military supporters on Capitol Hill that, were a larger sequester to come to pass in 1987, defense programs which they supported would take second place to an SDI program whose budget had tripled in its first three years. These pro-military, Congressional moderates, who had avoided the SDI debate in 1986, began to focus on some of the practical concerns being raised by experts familiar with SDI research. Throughout 1984 and 1985, House and Senate liberals had vigorously attacked the SDI program and the president's vision. The SDI budget request, however, suffered only modest reductions. Furthermore, the SDI debate on Capitol Hill had been largely ideological in that it pitted liberals who advocated deterrence and arms control against conservatives who believed in mutual assured survival through SDI, leaving moderates on the sidelines. Soon, however, congressional moderates began to question both the philosophical and technological justifications for SDI. As with most expensive programs, concerns over money and priorities began to converge.

SDI FUNDING DEBATE

Until 1986, the SDI funding debate had been unlike that over other military programs. In return for largely promises of a future in which Soviet nuclear weapons would be impotent, huge increases in the funding of ballistic missile defense research had been granted. No other major military program that claimed to be little more than applied research had seen increases of this size and proportion.

Moreover, the SDI Organization was reluctant to provide Congress with any meaningful milestones to measure its progress. Normally, each DoD research program is evaluated on the basis of its schedule and plan. Schedules and plans were fuzzy in the case of SDI, because they were defined largely by the vision of the President.

SDI also became a program of competing agendas. Some SDI enthusiasts advocated quick deployment of space-based kinetic kill vehicles. Others pushed for a concentration on ground-based lasers. Still others, such as Dr. Edward Teller of the Lawrence Livermore Laboratory, pushed for the so-called "pop-up" X-ray laser. Early on, Teller had criticized the space-based kinetic kill vehicle because of his conviction that such weapons could not be made survivable.

Furthermore, General Abrahamson's SDI Organization had been superimposed upon bureaucracies with their own views of the SDI. The Army Ballistic Missile Defense Command (now renamed the Strategic Defense Command) had been the primary agency conducting antiballistic missile research since the signing of the ABM treaty; however, its competition now included the Air Force Space Command. As expected, the Army and the Air Force had different ideas of what an SDI design might resemble. The SDI Organization, therefore, had to structure a program among competing interests of scientists, researchers, contractors, and established military bureaucracies.

Even by the standards of the expanding Reagan defense budgets of the 1980s, the $5.4 billion FY 1987 SDI request was enormous. Just three years earlier, ballistic missile defense research had been funded at less than $1 billion annually. Pressured by a popular president, who argued that an increase in SDI funding would guarantee success in the Geneva arms talks, Congress by FY1986 had tripled the SDI budget to about $3 billion. During the first year of Gramm-Rudman-Hollings, the administration asked Congress for another huge funding increase for SDI to $5.4 billion for FY 1987.

Critics of the program argued that there was no compelling justification for such an increase. The Soviets were not poised to break out of the ABM treaty. They contended that while SDI research had enjoyed successes, none of it was of a magnitude to justify redoubling the program budget. Some in Congress also noted that the FY 1987 SDI budget, if approved, would equal the entire research budget of the U.S. Army.

General Abrahamson, appearing to be sensitive to these realities, declared in the latter part of 1985 that there were "tremendous breakthroughs" being made in the research program. It was in response to these statements that Senators Proxmire, Johnston, and Chiles directed their staffs to review the SDI program. This was not an undifferentiated group. Senator Proxmire had long been a forceful and articulate advocate of arms control. Senators Johnston and Chiles were highly regarded pro-defense moderates who in large part had supported the administration's military modernization program. As noted earlier, most of this book is drawn from staff reviews conducted by the three authors.

SDI SCIENTISTS

Our studies revealed that there was a division of opinion between administration officials touting SDI "breakthroughs" and the scientists actually conducting the research. The scientists were virtually unanimous: SDI research was necessary, positive, and worthwhile, but there had been no "tremendous breakthroughs." The final solutions to very difficult physics and engineering problems were well over a decade away at best, they said.

The scientists' concerns, which our report publicized in March 1986, further fueled congressional concerns about the SDI program. If there were no extraordinary breakthroughs, why the greatly expanded budget requests? What about the ambitious development schedule that anticipated a full-scale engineering decision in the early 1990s? What impact would it have on the ABM treaty? Why, if we were at least a decade away from the point at which we might make an intelligent decision about an SDI deployment, were we pressing ahead with early demonstrations of hardware at such a furious pace? What innovative technologies would be sacrificed for the hurry-up schedule? What effect would these enormous budget increases have on other military programs?

THE SENATE

By spring 1986, the SDI debate had begun to intensify. After the release of our senate staff report, *SDI: Progress and Challenges*, which revealed that the claims of tremendous breakthroughs were disputed within SDI as well as outside the program, the lines began to harden. Congress had a budgetary goal set by the Gramm-Rudman-Hollings legislation. The Senate budget resolution was being debated and it appeared that the president's defense request would be reduced at least by $20 billion, which would leave the Pentagon with only enough increase to cover inflation. The question became, how could Congress reach its goals and still provide a 77% funding increase for the SDI?

This was the dilemma that the Senate Armed Services Committee faced. Under the leadership of Republican Chairman Barry Goldwater (R-Ariz.) and Senator San Nunn (D-Ga.), the committee had begun work early that year and on a 98-0 vote had passed landmark legislation to reorganize the Defense Department. Now the committee was preparing to approve the FY 1987 budget.

On May 22, 1986, however, 46 senators sent a letter to Goldwater and Nunn calling for no more than a three percent real growth in the SDI budget for FY 1987. On June 2, two more senators (for a total of 48) endorsed the principles enumerated by their colleagues.

The May 22 letter supported a robust SDI program based on innovative technologies; however, the senators insisted that SDI could not be considered separate from other military research efforts. They argued for a more realistic schedule and a "more evenly paced and broadbased SDI program...." It was clear that a significant number of senators believed that "budget growth" in the SDI had outpaced the progress of technology and had "begun to impinge on other military research and development." The letter, therefore, argued that considering its recent funding history and the general plight of other military programs, SDI should not receive more than a three percent real dollar increase over its FY 1986 budget.

The correspondence arrived as the Armed Services Committee prepared to move to closed session for completion of the FY 1987 Defense Authorization Bill. Immediately the concerns expressed in the May 22 letter, and elsewhere, had an effect on the committee. On July 8, 1986, the Committee issued its report on the FY87 Defense Bill. Working closely with Senator William Cohen (R-Maine), Senator Nunn had formulated a compromise that reduced the SDI request from $5.4 billion to $3.9 billion. More importantly, the committee proposed a Balanced Technology Initiative.

The report called for the SDI to be "refocused" according to four principles. First, it acknowledged the role SDI had in promoting an understanding of the "nature and pace of Soviet research on strategic defenses, especially research on 'exotic' technologies." Second, the report repeated its belief that SDI research should be directed "to hedge against the possibility of a Soviet ABM 'breakout' in the near term." Third, it recognized the daunting task SDI would have if its goal remained a comprehensive population defense. Accordingly, the report noted that, "issues such as effective midcourse discrimination and the ability of computer software to perform the necessary battle management functions remain to be resolved." Therefore, the report instructed the Defense Department to place primary emphasis not on an astrodome shield but rather on technologies "dedicated to developing survivable and cost effective defensive options for enhancing the survivability of U.S. retaliatory forces and command, control and communications systems."

Finally, the report played the so-called "Geneva card." While asserting SDI had provided some leverage to U.S. arms control negotiators in Geneva, it flatly stated that this leverage was derived from "real defense programs based on realistic objectives, adequately funded, and broadly supported by a bipartisan consensus." Most importantly, the report observed that "negotiating leverage is sometimes a perishable commodity." It suggested that, "we should be prepared to consider adjustments to the pace and scope of SDI if the Soviet Union agrees to significant stabilizing and verifiable reductions in strategic offensive forces."

In proposing a Balanced Technology Initiative, the report asserted that "the Administration's fiscal years 1987-91 funding profile for the SDI is excessive in light of the absence of basic architectures for this program and continuing indications of basic disagreements within the Administration as to the program's goals." Therefore the Committee, recognizing the negative effect SDI's funding growth was having on conventional research, directed that $490 million in SDI money be shifted to conventional research initiatives, "in areas such as armor/anti-armor..., smart mines..., stand-off munitions and submarines."

In effect, the Armed Services Committee had concluded that it had little confidence in the current direction of the SDI program. However, the funding reduction and the report language was not accomplished easily. It narrowly passed the committee on a 12-10 vote.

The FY 1987 Defense Bill came before the Senate in August 1986. The so-called "great debate" on SDI occupied the first two days of the session. An amendment whose principal co-sponsors were Senators Johnston, Proxmire, and Daniel Evans (R-Wash.), which would have further reduced SDI funding to $3.2 billion or a three percent growth level, failed by just one vote. For the SDI Organization, there was little room for rejoicing in that one-vote victory. The Armed Services Committee of the Republican-controlled Senate had substantially reduced its funding and had rejected its pursuit of the president's vision. Moreover, the full Senate in accepting the committee's language had rejected the "astrodome" defense. The Senate gave notice that SDI would now receive the same close scrutiny accorded other important defense programs. The House was next to act.

THE HOUSE

In the past, the Democratic-controlled House had been much more critical of SDI than the Senate and had voted lower funding levels. In 1986, however, the Senate had become more critical than the House of the president's vision for strategic defense. The Senate also led the House by organizing early its coalition of 48

Senators to limit SDI funding at no more than $3.2 billion for FY 1987.

The early Senate criticism of SDI provided a political shot in the arm for the House. With close to a majority of the Republican-controlled Senate favoring a $3.2 billion budget for SDI, Democratic House members felt they could push through a lower funding level. The House ultimately did just that as its Democratic leadership led a successful effort to approve just $3.1 billion for SDI. Moreover, the SDI funding level became part of a package of arms control measures, which the House approved to halt nuclear and anti-satellite weapons testing and to force the administration to remain in compliance with the U.S.-Soviet SALT II agreement.

Congress finally approved a funding level of $3.5 billion for SDI in FY 1987, splitting the difference between the $3.9 billion sought by the Senate and $3.1 billion approved by the House. This compromise emerged, along with compromise provisions substituting for the House's strict arms control requirements, during October 1986, shortly before President Reagan's meeting with Secretary Gorbachev in Reykjavik, Iceland.

NEAR-TERM DEPLOYMENT

After the FY 1987 Defense Appropriation bill passed Congress in the fall of 1986, and soon after the Reagan-Gorbachev summit in Reykjavik, a small group of SDI's more ardent supporters within the administration, the Congress, and private institutions began publicly calling for a "near-term" deployment of strategic defenses. Apparently there was a deepening concern among SDI proponents that the program was losing political momentum because its research objectives were too far in the future to compel large funding increases in the present. That slippage, it was feared, would continue unless SDI produced something identifiable, such as strategic defense hardware, around which Congress and the American public could rally.

This concern was perhaps best articulated in an October 1, 1986, letter to President Reagan and signed by some of SDI's strongest supporters: Rep. Jack Kemp, Rep. Jim Courter, Sen.

Rudy Boschwitz, Eugene V. Rostow, Dr. Edward Teller, and Dr. Lowell Wood. That letter, which called for "employment in the very near term of the most modern defensive means," stated:

> We are deeply concerned that a SDI program which has no definite consequences for a defense of America within the next ten years will not be politically sustainable.... We believe that imperfect but significant defensive options have already been laid before the American leadership by the SDI, and that they must not only be continued toward perfection but also prudently exercised, while the political will to do so undeniably exists.

Administration officials in the past had resisted premature deployment as damaging to SDI's overall goals. On August 6, 1986, President Reagan made this point to a group of SDI supporters:

> I know there are those who are getting a bit antsy, but to deploy systems of limited effectiveness now would divert limited funds and delay our main research. It could well erode support for the program before it's permitted to reach its potential.

By the end of 1986, however, a number of high administration officials began publicly advocating near-term deployment and pressuring the president for his formal approval. Secretary of Defense Caspar Weinberger has taken the lead in this effort. On January 12, 1987, before the Senate Armed Services Committee, Weinberger stated that it is "quite possible" that part of SDI will be deployed when it is ready rather than waiting for the full system to be perfected. Ten days later, in a Colorado Springs speech, Weinberger reiterated that,

> Today, we may be nearing the day when decisions about deployment of the first phase can be made. We are now seeing opportunities for earlier deployment of the first phase of strategic defense than we previously thought possible...our bags are packed.

Attorney General Edwin Meese, speaking at the Yale Club in January 1987, said President Reagan should move quickly to deploy the first stage of SDI "so it will be in place and not tampered with by future Administrations."

In early 1987, there was intense speculation that a presidential decision was imminent which would put near-term deployment into motion. As of this writing, no such decision has been publicly announced; furthermore, little information has been made public as to what shape a near-term deployment would take or what would be required to launch such an effort.

Several advocates outside the administration have offered their visions of a near-term deployment. In October 1986, the Heritage Foundation proposed deploying 100 upgraded missile interceptors over five years, and projected its cost to be $3.5 billion. While such a deployment presumably would be in compliance with the ABM treaty, it would have only token effectiveness against, perhaps, a stray Soviet ICBM missile.

Also last October, High Frontier, a pro-Star Wars organization, proposed a "ground up" near-term deployment consisting of ERIS interceptors, cloud guns, and space-based kinetic kill vehicles. The system supposedly would take up to seven-and-one-half years to deploy and cost some $30 billion. Recently the Department of Defense, in response to a request by Senator Johnston, made public its 1982 internal analyses of the High Frontier proposal. One such analysis estimated the proposal's cost to be $300 billion.

In December 1986, the newly formed George C. Marshall Institute issued a near-term deployment report, which it claimed was drawn from an "up-to-date data base" provided by SDI's program managers. The Marshall Institute report claimed that if a deployment decision were made in 1987, by 1994 the U.S. could begin deploying 11,000 space-based interceptors and 13,000 ground-based interceptors at a cost of $121 billion.

Based on our review of the reorientation under way in the SDI program and the tasks assigned to its contractors, we believe the near-term deployment SDIO has in mind for 1994-1995 would destroy no more than 16% of attacking Soviet ballistic missile warheads. Such a deployment in 1994-1995 would have: (a) no laser or beam weapons, as are popularly associated with SDI; (b) a token deployment of space-based kinetic kill vehicles in the boost phase that would destroy only about 11% of the rising Soviet missiles; (c) little or no midcourse kill or discrimination capability; and (d) 400 to 1,000 ground-based interceptors, produced on a hurry-up schedule, that might destroy no more than 5% of the incoming warheads.

One other point must be considered. Many advocates assume that a near-term deployment could be easily accomplished; however, they are seriously mistaken. A review of the technologies being considered for near-term deployment reveal they face tremendous engineering and production problems that will require a sizeable amount of research talent and substantial additional funding to overcome.

It remains to be seen whether the president will formally decide to proceed with a near-term deployment. It also remains to be seen whether Congress would appropriate funds for such a deployment. Many members of the House and Senate who have previously supported SDI appeared to have done so because they felt it was essentially a research program at this point. If the administration seeks to launch a near-term deployment, it is not clear whether these members would support moving from SDI research to SDI construction.

To summarize, there has been broad bipartisan support in Congress for a robust ballistic missile defense research program funded at much higher levels than in past years. But there has been little congressional support for a technology-limited research effort, or "crash program" as it has been more aptly called.

Chapter 6

Conclusions

As a result of our extensive interviews and briefings conducted with top SDIO officials, scientists, and outside experts, this study comes to the following conclusions:

(1) Congress should maintain a certain degree of skepticism toward claims of tremendous advances in SDI research. Hard questions should be asked about what any so-called "spectacular breakthroughs" have really accomplished and how far the research has actually advanced compared to the task at hand. So far, SDI has moved ahead by inches, while we still have miles to go.

(2) A closer look should be taken at whether boost-phase intercept can ever be effective and whether space-based assets can ever be made survivable. If the evidence shows that boost-phase intercept cannot work and space-based assets cannot be protected, with or without arms control, serious questions should be raised about the feasibility of implementing the president's vision of a comprehensive strategic defense.

(3) The problem of discriminating warheads from decoys in the midcourse phase of defense is much larger than Congress has been led to believe. SDIO is just beginning to address this problem.

(4) Congress should be concerned about the priority shifts SDIO has made in its program. They appear to indicate that, contrary to public pronouncements, SDIO still does not have a firm idea of how a strategic defense system might be implemented. Nevertheless, Congress is being asked to pour billions of dollars

into the program based on assumptions that the direction of the program is clear.

(5) Congress should question why SDIO is rushing to arrive at a development decision by the early 1990s. Comprehensive ballistic missile defenses would not become fully operational until nearly two decades from now. Congress should be fully aware of the serious risks involved in making a premature decision on whether to develop strategic defenses. Moreover, Congress should inquire as to whether additional time for research will result in a sounder development decision.

(6) Congress should question any move toward an early deployment of strategic defenses. A near-term deployment in the 1994-1995 time frame could not be easily accomplished. And because of its very limited capability, a near-term deployment would not significantly enhance U.S. security and would only serve as a somewhat complicating factor for Soviet attack plans. Congress should examine carefully whether such a deployment is worth (a) the significant costs that would be incurred, (b) the likely termination of the ABM treaty, and (c) the deep divisions it likely will cause between the U.S. and its allies.

(7) So far, Congressional debate over SDI has centered largely on its national security implications and on whether strategic defenses are militarily feasible. Much more scrutiny, however, must be given to whether it is feasible to produce, deploy and maintain such a system. It may well be that the production, transportation, support, logistics, and administrative requirements of a strategic defense system are as tremendous as the military and technical requirements.

(8) A closer look should be taken at current and future U.S.-Soviet arms control regimes and their relationship with SDI. Proposals to dismantle SALT, if implemented, would only make SDI's task more difficult. Abandoning the ABM treaty now would only leave the Soviet Union with an advantage for the near-term in the deployment of hard-point defenses. The evidence indicates that further arms control constraints on the Soviet Union are necessary in order to make strategic defenses feasible. The question remains, however, whether such an arms control regime can be established.

(9) After completing this review of the SDI research and the defensive systems being envisioned, we are struck by myriad uncertainties and unknowns at every turn in the program—uncertainties and unknowns that bear directly on the effectiveness of future strategic defenses. And much of that uncertainty likely will remain, for even with strategic defenses in place, the U.S. would never be able to adequately test the system under realistic conditions.

SDI supporters cite Soviet uncertainty as a rationale for deploying SDI. The Soviets would be deterred from attacking the U.S. because of their uncertainty over how well they could overcome U.S. defenses. However, if the Soviets deploy their own defensive system, which the president has invited them to do, then both they and we would likely be uncertain about the effectiveness of both *our* and *their* systems.

It would seem inevitable that faced with these uncertainties, both the U.S. and U.S.S.R. would deem it necessary to maintain a highly secure and effective anti-satellite capability to ensure that at the onset of a nuclear conflict they did not suddenly discover their adversary's defense intact and their own defense in disarray. Thus, both sides would have strategic defenses in place with separate ASAT weapons poised to destroy the other's defense system. This situation does not strike us as a stable environment for the future.

Furthermore, it is disturbing that despite more than a tripling of its budget over the past four years, the SDIO has been unable or unwilling to develop any cost estimate for deployment and maintenance of a comprehensive strategic defense system. SDIO's statement that it will estimate what these defenses *should* cost is not enough. Congress needs to know what these defenses *will* cost.

(10) Finally, this report has examined only the progress and challenges of SDI research. It leaves open any detailed examination of whether strategic defenses are desirable even if some or many of the challenges can be overcome.

Congress and the public, therefore, may wish to consider six important questions.

— Can strategic defenses, particularly those intercepting ballistic missiles in the boost-phase, be made survivable in the face of future Soviet offensive threats and countermeasures.

— Can effective discrimination be achieved in the midcourse phase of defense to distinguish Soviet warheads from decoys, which, all told, may number in the millions during an attack?

— Why is it so important to make a development decision on the Strategic Defense Initiative by the early 1990s if that decision will be so fraught with risks?

— Should the SDI program be reorientated to pursue vigorously a near-term deployment of strategic defenses?

— What are the implications for SDI research overall and for U.S. national security if a reorientation toward near-term strategic defenses proceeds?

— What will it cost not only to deploy strategic defenses, but also to maintain such a system?

Chapter 7

References

Preparing oneself to engage the controversies swirling about the SDI program and to intelligently sort out a reasonable position is not easily done. Much of the "strategic" literature which deals with broad political-military issues often carry an almost theological cast since nearly all of the propositions are not verifiable. Consequently, these studies reflect the authors' basic assumptions about the motives of the Soviets or Americans. Thus the novice (as well as the strategist) would do well to first read (or reread) Freeman Dyson's *Weapons and Hope* (New York: Harper, 1984) and Bernard Brodie's *War and Politics* (New York: Macmillan, 1973). These two books deal with the broader issues and provide a perspective within which one may wrestle profitably with SDI issues. Neither author confuses the roles of generals and diplomats—both are needed, but while generals may gain victories, only diplomats can achieve peace. As this study does not attempt to address every issue regarding the SDI debate, these bibliographical citations will assist the serious researcher in gaining the fullest possible view of the controversy. The titles have been arranged under various categories in order to provide prompt access to references related to specific themes or issues. The decision as where to list an individual title was, obviously, arbitrary and—since most accounts examine several different topics—one should carefully review related categories.

Also, this is a selective collection of references. Under some headings we have indicated that our citations constitute only a sampling of available references. This is particularly true when introducing such wide-ranging topics as "arms control," "deterrence," and "nuclear strategy." Due to limitations of space we have included few newspaper or popular magazine articles, yet these are often informative. For access to additional titles, review the bibliographies listed under *References*, immediately below. A reader wishing to up-date this list may do so by consulting *Arms Control Today* and *Public Affairs Information Service* (PAIS) which lists articles, books and documents; or *ABC POL SCI* and *Readers Guide* which list articles.

This bibliographic essay was prepared jointly by the authors and the Center for the Study of Armament and Disarmament, California State University, Los Angeles. The very considerable efforts of Michael Haussler, a Center research associate, in locating many of these titles is acknowledged here with gratitude.

REFERENCE GUIDES

Lawrence's research guide (5) contains references not mentioned here; Marshall and Scott (7) provide additional collateral references; and historical dimensions may be searched through Burns (2). Champion (3) provides references to the literature on space weaponry; while Long, Hafner and Boutwell (6) provide descriptions of these systems.

1   Arms Control Association. *Star Wars Quotes: Statements by Reagan Administration Officials, Outside Experts, Members of Congress, U.S. Allies, and Soviet Officials on the Strategic Defense Initiative.* Washington, D.C.: Arms Control Assoc., July 1986.

2   Burns, Richard Dean. *Arms Control and Disarmament: A Bibliography.* Santa Barbara, CA: ABC-Clio, 1977. (historical dimensions of several issues)

3   Champion, Brian. *Advanced Weapons Systems: An Annotated Bibliography of the Cruise Missile, MX Missile, Laser and Space Weapons, and Stealth Technology.* New York: Garland, 1985.

4   Kruzel, Joseph, ed. *American Defense Annual, 1986-1987.* Lexington, MA: Lexington Books, 1986.

5   Lawrence, Robert M. *Strategic Defense Initiative: Bibliography and Research Guide.* Boulder, CO.: Westview, 1987.

6   Long, Franklin A., Donald Hafner and Jeffrey Boutwell, eds. *Weapons in Space*. New York: Norton, 1986.

7   Marshall, Charles W., comp. and Kathleen Scott, ed. *Selected Bibliography of Contemporary Strategic Issues*. Guelph, Ontario (Canada): University of Guelph, Office for Educational Practice, 1985. (includes material on SDI and BMD, SALT, START and INF)

Documents

These references provide a considerable amount of data relating to the administration's views of SDI. Other documents appear throughout under specific topics. Researchers seeking DoD documents may telephone its Public Affairs Office at (202) 697-6462 for assistance.

8   *The Strategic Defense Initiative: Defensive Technologies Study.*[Fletcher Report]. Washington, D.C.: DoD, Mar. 1984.

9   Department of Defense. *Defense Against Ballistic Missiles: An Assessment of Technologies and Policy Implications*. Washington, D.C.: DoD, Apr. 1984.

10   Department of Defense. *Overview of Strategic Defense Initiative: Fact Sheet*. Washington, D.C.: DoD, Mar. 9, 1984.

11   Department of Defense. *Report to the Congress on the Strategic Defense Initiative*. Washington, D.C.: G.P.O., 1985.

12   Department of Defense. *Report to the Congress on the Strategic Defense Initiative*. Washington, D.C.: G.P.O., June 1986.

13   Department of Defense. *The Strategic Defense Initiative: Defensive Technologies Study*. Washington, D.C.: G.P.O., Apr. 1984.

14   Department of State. *The Strategic Defense Initiative*. Special Report no. 129. Washington, D.C.: G.P.O., 1985.

15   House. Committee on Foreign Affairs. Subcommittee on Arms Control, Hearings; International Security and Science. *Implications of the President's Strategic Defense Initiative and Anti-Satellite Weapons Policy*. Washington, D.C.: G.P.O., Apr. 24 and May 1, 1985.

16   House. Committee on Government Operations. Hearings; *Our Nation's Nuclear Warning System: Will it Work If We Need It?* Washington, D.C.: G.P.O., 1986.

Reagan's Position

Listed are statements made by, or attributed to, President Reagan from 1983 to 1986. A search of the *Weekly Compilation of Presidential Documents* will reveal more.

17 "President Ronald Reagan's Address to the Nation, March 23, 1983: 'Peace and National Security'." *Daedalus* 114 (Summer 1985), Appendix B: Relevant Documents, pp. 369-372.

18 "The President's Strategic Defense Initiative, Jan. 3, 1985." *Survival* 27 (Mar./Apr. 1985), 79-82. Excerpts Administration publication released Jan. 3, 1985 in conjunction with U.S.-Soviet talks in Geneva on Jan. 7-8. (U.S.'s rationale for SDI)

19 Reagan, Ronald. "Strategic Defense Initiative: Radio Address to the Nation, July 13, 1985." *Weekly Compilation of Presidential Documents* (July 22, 1985), 901-902.

20 Reagan, Ronald. *SDI: Progress and Promise.* Current Policy No. 858. Washington, D.C.: U.S. Department of State, Bureau of Public Affairs, Aug. 1986.

21 White House. *The President's Strategic Defense Initiative.* Washington, D.C.: G.P.O., Jan. 1985. (reiterates Reagan's position)

SDI: GENERAL

DiMaggio, et.al. (33), The Aspin Study Group (23,24), Stone (58) and Young (63) provide overviews of various SDI issues. Smoke (38) and Stein (39) put SDI in historical and strategic perspective.

Books

22 Armstrong, Scott and Peter Grier. *Strategic Defense Initiative: Splendid Defense or Pipe Dream?* New York: Foreign Policy Assoc., 1986.

23 The Aspen Study Group. *Key Issues in American Security: Anti-Satellite Weapons and U.S. Military Space Policy.* Lanham, MD.: University Press of America, 1985.

24 The Aspen Study Group. *The Strategic Defense Initiative and American Security.* Lanham, MD.: University Press of America, 1986.

25 Binnendyk, Hans, ed. *Strategic Defense in the 21st Century.* Washington, D.C.: U.S. Department of State, Center for the Study of Foreign Affairs, Foreign Service Institute, 1986.

26   Bosma, John T. and Richard C. Whelan. *Guide to the Strategic Defense Initiative*. Arlington, VA: Pasha, 1985 and 1986. (broad study of program elements with in SDIO)

27   Bova, Ben. *Assured Survival: Putting the Star Wars Defense in Perspective*. Boston: Houghton Mifflin, 1984.

28   Brauch, Hans Gunter, ed. *From "Star Wars" to Strategic Defense Initiative*. New York: St. Martins', 1986.

29   Brzezinski, Zbigniew, ed. *Promise or Peril: The Strategic Defense Initiative*. Washington, D.C.: Ethics & Public Policy Center, 1986.

30   Cimbala, Stephen J., ed. *The Strategic Defense Initiative: Technology, Strategy, and Politics*. Boulder, CO.: Westview, 1987.

31   Deudney, Daniel. *Whole Earth Security: A Geopolitics of Peace*. No. 55. Washington, D.C.: Worldwatch Institute, 1983. (Star Wars and other security problems)

32   DiMaggio, Cosmo, and Davey Michael. *The Strategic Defense Initiative Institute: An Assessment of DoD's Current Proposal*. Washington, D.C.: Congressional Research Service, Library of Congress, Aug. 1986.

33   DiMaggio, Cosmo, Arthur F. Manfredi, and Steven A. Hildreth. *The Strategic Defense Initiative, Program Description and Major Issues*. Washington, D.C.: Congressional Research Service, Library of Congress, Jan. 7, 1986.

34   Guertner, Gary L., and Donald M. Snow. *The Last Frontier: An Analysis of the Strategic Defense Initiative*. Lexington, MA: Lexington Books, 1986. (good survey)

35   Hadley, Stephen J. *Thinking About SDI*. Washington, D.C.: Foreign Policy Institute, School of Advanced International Studies, Johns Hopkins University, 1986.

36   Haley, P. Edward and Jack Merritt, eds. *Strategic Defense: Folly or Future?* Boulder, CO: Westview, 1986.

37   Kent, Glenn A. and Randall J. DeValk. *Strategic Defense and the Transition to Assured Survival*. Santa Monica, CA: RAND Corp., Oct. 1986.

38   Smoke, Richard. *National Security and the Nuclear Dilemma: An Introduction to the American Experience*. 2nd. ed. New York: Random House, 1987. (esp. Ch. 13; puts SDI in perspective)

39   Stein, Jonathan. *From H-Bomb to Star Wars: The Politics of Strategic Decision Making*. Lexington, MA: Lexington Books, 1984.

40   Vlahos, Michael. *Strategic Defense and and the American Ethos: Can the Nuclear World be Changed?* Boulder, CO: Westview for the Foreign Policy Institute, School of Advanced International Studies, Johns Hopkins University, 1986.

Articles

41   Arkin, William M. "Of Drugs and Star Wars." *Bulletin of the Atomic Scientists* 42 (Feb. 1986), 4-5.

42   Black, Edwin F. "Assured Mutual Survival: The ABM Solution." *Journal of Social, Political and Economic Studies* 9 (Summer 1984), 141-143.

43   Blackaby, F. "The Strategic Defense Initiative and Its Implications." *Bulletin of Peace Proposals* 17:3/4 (1986),323-330.

44   Brown, Neville. "SDI: The Cardinal Questions." *World Today* 42 (May 1986), 81-83.

45   Brown, Paul S. "Why Research on Defensive Weapons is Important." *Scientia* 120 (Oct. 1985), 349-359.

46   Codevilla, Angelo. "Understanding Ballistic Missile Defense." *Journal of Contemporary Studies* (Winter 1984), 19-34.

47   Dahlite, Julie. "The Option of Star Wars." *Bulletin of Peace Proposals* 16:2 (1985), 99-104.

48   Guertner, Gary L. "Strategic Defense: New Technologies, Old Tactics." *Parameters: Journal of the U.S. Army War College* 15 (Autumn 1985), 16-22.

49   Guertner, Gary L. "What is 'Proof'?" *Foreign Policy* no. 59 (Summer 1985), 73-84. (plea for a non-polemical review of SDI issues)

50   Jones, Rodney W. and Steven A. Hildreth. "Star Wars: Down to Earth or Gleam in the Sky." *Washington Quarterly* 7 (Fall 1984), 104-111.

51   Kubbig, Bernd W. "Spin-off and the Strategic Defense Initiative: Promises, Premises, and Problems." *Bulletin of Peace Proposals* 17:2 (1986), 159-163.

52   *Millenium: Journal of International Studies* 15 (Summer 1986). (entire issue devoted to strategy and arms control; SDI articles are individually referenced here)

53   Morrison, David C. "ICBM Vulnerability." *Bulletin of Atomic Scientists* 40 (Nov. 1984), 22-29.

54   Richardson, Robert C. III. "Security in the Nuclear Age: A New Strategy in Space." *Journal of Social, Political and Economic Studies* 9 (Summer 1984), 198-210.

55   Richardson, Robert C. III. "Star Wars: Some Less Frequently Discussed Considerations." *Journal of Social, Political and Economic Studies* 10 (Summer 1985), 131-154.

56   Ruina, Jack. "Perspectives on the Strategic Defense Initiative." *Scientia* 120 (Oct. 1985), 427-430.

57   Schlesinger, James R. "Speech on Ballistic Missile Defense at Symposium on Space, National Security and C-cubed-I." Bedford, MA: Mitre Corporation, Oct. 25, 1984. Mitre Document M85-3, 55-62.

58 Stone, Jeremy. "The Four Faces of Star Wars: Anatomy of a Debate." *F.A.S. Public Interest Report: Journal of the Federation of American Scientists* 38 (March 1985), 1-9.

59 Waller, Douglas; James Bruce; and Douglas Cook. "Star Wars: Breakthrough or Breakdown?" *Arms Control Today* 16 (May/June 1986), 8-12.

60 "Weapons in Space." Vol. I: "Concepts and Technologies." *Daedalus* 114 (Spring 1985), 17-192. (entire issue devoted to SDI; each article is referenced here)

61 "Weapons in Space."Vol. II: "Implications for Security." *Daedalus* 114 (Summer 1985), 193-397. (entire issue devoted to SDI; each article and appendice is referenced here)

62 Weinberg, Alvin M. and Jack N. Barkenbus. "Stabilizing Star Wars." *Foreign Policy* no. 54 (Spring 1984), 164-170. (offers an alternative policy)

63 Young, Alwyn. "Ballistic Missile Defense: Capabilities and Constraints." *Fletcher Forum* 8 (Winter 1984), 147-175. (good introduction to issues)

64 Zimmerman, Peter D. "Pork Bellies and SDI." *Foreign Policy* 63 (Summer 1986), 76-87.

HISTORICAL PERSPECTIVE

The historical controversy over deployment is charted in Yanarella (75) and Lin (71); while Carter and Schwartz (73) also provides background information. See also ABM Treaty & SDI, below, for additional materials.

65 Adams, Benson D. *Ballistic Missile Defense.* New York: American Elsevier, 1971.

66 Adams, Benson D. "Strategy and the First Strategic Defense Initiative." *Naval War College Review* 37 (Nov.-Dec. 1985), 50-58. (Britain's decision for fighters and radar in the 1930s)

67 Chayes, Abram and Jerome B. Wiesner., eds. *ABM.* New York: Harper & Row, 1969. (the first Ballistic Missile Defense controversy)

68 Flax, Alexander. "Ballistic Missile Defense: Concepts and History." *Daedalus* 114 (Spring 1985), 33-52.

69 Halperin, Morton H. "The Decision to Deploy the ABM: Bureaucratic and Domestic Politics in the Johnson Administration." *World Politics* 25:1 (1972), 62-95.

70　Jayne, Edward R. *The ABM Debate: Strategic Defense and National Security.* Cambridge: MIT, Center for Strategic Studies, 1969. (see also his Ph.D. dissertation)

71　Lin, Herbert. *Ballistic Missile Defense: Then and Now.* Ithaca, NY: Cornell University, Peace Studies Program, Oct. 22, 1983.

72　Schneider, William, Jr., et al. *The Strategic Nuclear Policy and Ballistic Missile Defense: The 1980s and Beyond.* Cambridge, MA: Institute for Foreign Policy Analysis, 1980.

73　Schwartz, David N. "Past and Present: The Historical Legacy." In *Ballistic Missile Defense.* Washington, D.C. Brookings Institutions, 1984.

74　Slater, Jerome. "Re-examining the ABM Moratorium: Population Defense Reconsidered; Is the ABM Really Inconsistent with Stability?" *Policy Studies Journal* 8:1 (1979), 53-59.

75　Yanarella, Ernest J. *The Missile Defense Controversy: Strategy, Technology, and Politics, 1955-1972.* Lexington: University Press of Kentucky, 1977. ("battles" over ballistic missile defense system)

COST OF SDI

Fiscal implications are examined by Blechman and Utgoff (77), Field and Spergel (79) and Pike (87). The competition for SDI research dollars is suggested by Alexander (76).

76　Alexander, Charles P. "The Star Wars Sweepstakes: Amid a Swirl of Controversy, Companies and Schools Vie for Defense Dollars." *Time* 128 (Oct. 7, 1985), 49-52.

77　Blechman, Barry M. and Victor A. Utgoff. *Fiscal and Economic Implications of Strategic Defenses.* Boulder, CO: Westview for the Foreign Policy Institute of Advanced of International Studies, Johns Hopkins University, 1986.

78　Blechman, Barry M., and Victor A. Utgoff. "The Macroeconomics of Strategic Defenses." *International Security* 11 (Winter 1986), 33-70. (abbreviated version of their book)

79　Field, George and David Spergel. "Cost of Space-Based Laser Ballistic Missile Defense." *Science* 222 (Mar. 21, 1986), 1387-1393.

80　Gollon, Peter J. "SDI Funds Costly for Scientists." *Bulletin of the Atomic Scientists* 42 (Jan. 1986), 24-26.

81　Goodwin, I. "Senators and Scientists Object to SDI Costs and Uncertainties." *Physics Today* 38 (July 1985), 55-59. (anti-SDI)

82   Hartung, William D., et al. *The Strategic Defense Initiative: Costs, Contractors and Consequences.* New York: Council on Economic Priorities, 1985.

83   Kozicharon, E. "Army Doubles Missile Defense Fund Bid to Support SDI Effort." *Aviation Week & Space Technology* 122 (Apr. 8, 1985), 62-63.

84   Mohr, Charles. "Chief of Missile Defense Project Seeks to Reshape Policy on Costs." *New York Times,* May 1, 1986.

85   Mohr, Charles. "Cost Cuts Sought in Missile Defense." *New York Times,* May 8, 1986.

86   Mohr, Charles. "GAO Says 2 Missile Defense Projects Were Cut to Meet Deadline." *New York Times,* July 17, 1986.

87   Pike, John. *The Strategic Defense Initiative Budget and Program.* Washington, D.C.: Federation of American Scientists, July 1985.

88   "Secretary of Defense Caspar W. Weinberger to the Congress, February 14, 1985, on the FY 1986 Budget, FY 1987 Authorization Request, and FY 1986-90. Defense Program: 'The Strategic Defense Initiative'." *Daedalus* 114 (Summer 1985), Appendix B: Relevant Documents, 373-378.

89   Sheppard, Eric. "Value and Exploitation in a Capitalist Space Economy." *International Regional Science Review* 9 (Nov. 1984), 97-108.

ETHICS, MORALITY AND SDI

The Philosophical Forum essays examine the administration's claim that SDI is a "moral" concept.

90   Kanka, Gregory S. "Space War Ethics." *Ethics* 95 (Apr. 1985), 673-691.

91   Kramer, Ken. "Space and New Strategic Ethics." *Space World* 25 (May 1983), 2-3.

92   Lee, Steven. "The Moral Vision of Strategic Defense." *Philosophical Forum* 18 (Fall 1986), 15-21. (critical)

93   Lackey, Douglas P. "Moral Principles and Strategic Defense." *Philosophical Forum* 18 (Fall 1986), 1-7.

94   McGrath, Mary Eileen E. "Nuclear Weapons: A Crisis of Conscience." *Military Law Review* 107 (Winter 1985), 191-254.

95   Shue, Henry. "Morality of Offense Determines Morality of Defense." *Philosophical Forum* 18 (Fall 1986), 8-14. (doesn't take sides)

96   Valley, B.L. "The Morality and Psychology of Science." (Address, July 24, 1985) *Vital Speeches of the Day* 51 (Sept. 15, 1985), 732-736. (examines morality of SDI)

97   Weinberger, Caspar W. "Ethics and Public Policy: The Case of SDI."
      Fletcher Forum 10:1 (Winter 1986), 1-6.

LEGAL ISSUES

Chayes, Chayes and Spitzer (99) and Sherr (106) are good
sources to begin an examination of the legal issues. See also ABM
Treaty, Reagan Administration's Interpretation, below.

98   Arbess, Daniel. "Star Wars and Outer Space Laws." *Bulletin of the
      Atomic Scientists* 41 (Oct. 1985), 19-22.

99   Chayes, Abram and Antonia Handler Chayes, Eliot Spitzer. "Space
      Weapons: The Legal Context." *Daedalus* 114 (Summer 1985), 193-
      218.

100   Feinrider, Martin. "The Strategic Defense Initiative and International
      Law." *Fletcher Forum* 10 (Winter 1986), 19-32.

101   Gallagher, Michael G. "Legal Aspects of the Strategic Defense Initiative."
      Military Law Review III (Winter 1986), 11-48.

102   Goldblat, Jozef. "New Means of Ballistic Missile Defense: The Questions
      of Legality and Arms Control Implications." *Arms Control and
      Disarmament* 5 (Sept. 1984), 176-180.

103   Gorove, Stephan. "Expectations in Space Law: A Peek into the Future."
      Journal of International Affairs 39 (Summer 1985), 167-174.

104   Meredity, Pamela L. *The Legality of a High Technology Missile Defense
      System: The ABM and Outer Space Treaties.* Los Angeles: UCLA,
      Center for International Security and Arms Control, 1984.

105   Rosas, Allan. "The Militarization of Space and International Law."
      Journal of Peace Research 20:4 (1983), 57-64.

106   Sherr, Alan B. *Legal Issues of the "Star Wars" Defense Program.* Boston,
      MA: Lawyers Alliance for Nuclear Arms Control, June 1984.

107   Topping, John. "The Legality of President Reagan's Proposed Space-
      Based Ballistic Missile Defense System." *Georgia Journal of
      International and Comparative Law* 14 (Summer 1985), 329-356.

108   Zedalis, Rex J. "On the Lawfulness of Forceful Remedies for Violations of
      Arms Control Agreements: 'Star Wars' and Other Glimpses of the
      Future." *New York University Journal of International Law and
      Politics* 18 (Fall 1985), 73-168.

SDI DEBATE

The SDI debate has found the press doing its homework.
William Broad and Charles Mohr with the *New York Times,* Fred

Hiatt and Jeffrey Smith with the *Washington Post* have given particularly noteworthy coverage of the issue. Snyder (115) and the House hearings (116) contain pro and con views.

109 Ball, George. "The War for Star Wars." *New York Times Review of Books* (Apr. 11, 1985), 38-44.

110 Brown, Harold. "The Strategic Defense Initiative: Defensive Systems and the Strategic Debate." *Atlantaic Community Quarterly* 23 (Summer 1985), 143-156.

111 Brown, Harold. "Too Much, Too Soon." *Arms Control Today* 17:4 (1987), 2-3. (opposes early deployment)

112 Levine, Robert A. *The SDI Debate as a Continuation of History*. Los Angeles: Center for International and Strategic Affairs, University of California, Los Angeles, CSIA Working Paper #55, 1986.

113 Means, M.L., and J.F. Voss. "Star Wars: A Developmental Study of Expert and Novice Knowledge Structures." *Journal of Memory and Language* 24:6 (1985), 746-757.

114 Miller, Steven E. and Stephan van Evera, eds. *The Star Wars Controversy*. Princeton, NJ: Princeton University Press, 1986.

115 Snyder, Craig, ed. *The Strategic Defense Debate: Can "Star Wars" Make Us Safe?* Philadelphia: University of Pennsylvania Press, 1986. (essays pro and con)

116 House. Committee on Foreign Affairs. Subcommittee on International Security and Scientific Affairs. Hearings; *Arms Control in Outer Space*. Nov. 10, 1983; Apr. 10, May 2, and July 26, 1984. Washington, D.C.: G.P.O., 1984. (both sides air views)

117 Woolsey, R. James. "Memo For: SDI Supporters and Critics." *Armed Forces Journal International* 122 (Sept. 1985), 98-100.

SDI AND POLITICS

Hartung (122) suggests that SDI is becoming emerged in politics in part because defense contractors pressure congressmen and senators.

118 Codevilla, Angelo. "Understanding Ballistic Missile Defense." *Journal of Contemporary Studies* 7 (Winter 1984), 19-35. (supportive)

119 Garfinkle, Adam M. "The Politics of Space Defense." *Orbis* 28 (Summer 1984), 240-256.

120 Garrily, Patrick J. "The United States: The Politics of Strategic Defense." *World Today* 40 (Dec. 1984), 3-7.

121   Graham, Thomas W. and Bernard M. Kramer. "The Polls: ABM and Star
      Wars: Attitudes Toward Nuclear Defense, 1945-1985." *Public Opinion
      Quarterly* 50:1 (Spring 1986), 125-142. (public opinion poll on SDI)

122   Hartung, William. "Star Wars Pork Barrel." *Bulleting of the Atomic
      Scientists* 42 (Jan. 1986), 20-23. (defense contractors supporting SDI;
      have much influence in Congress)

123   Hoffman, Fred S. "The SDI in U.S. Nuclear Strategy: Senate Testimony."
      International Security 10:1 (1985), 13-24.

124   Pressler, Larry. *Star Wars: The Strategic Defense Initiative Debates in
      Congress.* New York: Praeger, 1986.

125   Vandercook, William F. "SDI Show Hits the Road." *Bulletin of the
      Atomic Scientists* 42 (Oct. 1986), 16-19.

126   Wayman, Frank Whelon. "Arms Control and Strategic Arms Voting in the
      U.S. Senate: Patterns of Change, 1967-1983." *Journal of Conflict
      Resolution* 29 (June 1985), 225-252.

SDI SCEPTICS & CRITICS

Opponents to SDI vary in their criticism. Carter and Schwartz
(128) provide a wide-ranging critique; former Air Force officer
Bowman (127) finds fault with SDI from a military perspective;
and Drell and Panofsky (142) are two of the scientific community's
most respected critics. Pike (147) serves as the loyal opposition's
most articulate pundit; while Garwin (144-147) is a passionate
representative of traditional deterrence and is a scathing critic.

Books

127   Bowman, Robert. *Star Wars: Defense or Death Star.* Potomac, MD:
      Institute for Space and Security Studies, 1985. (criticizes from a
      military point of view)

128   Carter, Ashton B. and David N. Schwartz, eds. *Ballistic Missile Defense.*
      Washington, D.C.: Brookings Institution, 1984.

129   Cunningham, Ann Marie, and Mariana Fitzpatrick. *Future Fire: Weapons
      for the Apocalypse.* New York: Warner, 1983. (see esp. chs. 5, 6, & 7)

130   Drell, Sidney D., Philip J. Farley; and David Holloway. *The Reagan
      Strategic Defense Initiative: A Technical, Political, and Arms Control
      Assessment.* Cambridge, MA: Ballinger, 1985. (printed earlier by the
      Center for International Security and Arms Control, Stanford
      University)

131   Drell, Sidney and Thomas H. Johnson, eds. *Strategic Missile Defense:
      Necessities, Prospects and Dangers in the Near Term.* Report of a

workshop at the Center for International Security and Arms Control, Stanford University, Apr. 1985.

132 Ennals, Richard. *Star Wars: A Question of Initiative*. New York: Wiley, 1987. (British view; anti-SDI)

133 Tirman, John, ed. *The Fallacy of Star Wars*. New York: Vintage, 1984.

134 Union of Concerned Scientists. *Star Wars: Myth and Reality*. Washington, D.C.: Union of Concerned Scientists, 1986.

Articles

135 Bethe, Hans A.; Richard L. Garwin; Kurt Gottfried; and Henry W. Kendall. "Space-based Ballistic Missile Defense." *Scientific American* 251 (Oct. 1984), 39-49.

136 Blacker, Coit D. "Defending Missiles, Not People: Hard-Site Defense." *Issues in Science and Technology* 2 (Fall 1985), 30-44.

137 Boutwell, Jeffrey and F.A. Long. "The SDI and U.S. Security." *Daedalus* 114 (Summer 1985), 315-330.

138 Burrows, William E. "Ballistic Missile Defense:The Illusion of Security." *Foreign Affairs* 62 (Spring 1984), 843-856.

139 Clausen, Peter A. "The SDI Debate: A Critic's Perspective." *Fletcher Forum* 10 (Winter 1986), 33-38.

140 Clausen, Peter A. "SDI in Search of a Mission." *World Policy Journal* 2 (Spring 1985), 249-303. (either SDI or arms control)

141 Dely, Alex. "Star Wars, False Alarms, and Accidental Nuclear War." *Peace Research Reviews* 10 (1986A), 47-57. ("Nuclear Time Bomb" issue, pt.2: suggests SDI could accidentally trigger nuclear war)

142 Drell, Sidney and Wolfgang K.H. Panofsky. "The Case Against Strategic Defense: Technical and Strategic Realities." *Issues in Science and Technology* 1 (Fall 1984), 45-65.

143 Deudney, Daniel. "Forging Missiles Into Spaceships." *World Policy Journal* 2 (Spring 1985), 271-303.

144 Garwin, Richard L. "Countermeasures: Defeating Space-based Defense." *Arms Control Today* 15 (May 1985), 2-3. (anti-SDI)

145 Garwin, Richard L. "How Many Orbiting Lasers for Boost-Phase Intercept?" *Nature* 314 (May 23, 1985), 286-290.

146 Garwin, Richard L. "Star Wars: Shield or Threat." *Journal of International Affairs* 39 (Summer 1985), 31-44.

147 Garwin, Richard L., John Pike, and Yevgeny P. Velikovo. "Space Weapons." *Bulletin of the Atomic Scientists* 40 (May 1984) (supplement).

148   Glaser, Charles L. "Do We Want the Missile Defenses We Can Build?" *International Security* 10 (Summer 1985), 25-27. (critical, prefers strength & ABM Treaty)

149   Glaser, Charles L. "Star Wars Bad Even if it Works." *Bulletin of the Atomic Scientists* 41 (Mar. 1985), 13-16.

150   Glen, Maxwell. "'Star Wars' Doubts." *National Journal* 17 (Aug. 10, 1985), 1832-1836.

151   Hafner, Donald L. "Assessing the President's Vision: The Fletcher, Miller, and Hoffman Panels." *Daedalus* 114 (Spring 1985), 91-108.

152   Holm, Hans-Henrik. "Star Wars." *Journal of Peace Research* 23 (Mar. 1986), 1-8.

153   Hoopes, Townsend. "The Star Wars Proposal." *CNS Reports.* The Committee for National Security. Washington, D.C., Winter 1985.

154   Kogut, John and Michael Weissman. "Taking the Pledge Against Star Wars." *Bulletin of the Atomic Scientists* 42 (Jan. 1986), 27-30.

155   Krauthammer, Charles. "The Illusion of Star Wars: The Worst Offense is a Bad Defense." *New Republic* 190 (May 14, 1984), 13-17. (good non-technical discussion)

156   Lebow, Richard Ned. "Assured Strategic Stupidity: The Quest for Ballistic Missile Defense." *Journal of International Affairs* 39 (Summer 1985), 57-80.

157   McNamara, Robert S. "Reducing the Risk of Nuclear War: Is Star Wars the Answer?" *Millenium: Journal of International Studies* 15 (Summer 1986), 133-142.

158   Marsh, Gerald E. "SDI: The Stability Question." *Bulletin of the Atomic Scientists* 41 (Oct. 1985), 23-25.

159   Morrison, David C. "Shooting Down Star Wars." *National Journal* 18 (Oct. 1986), 2544-2549.

160   Morrison, David C. "Star Wars Woes." *National Journal* 18 (July 12, 1986), 1726.

161   Panofsky, Wolfgang K.H. "The Strategic Defense Initiative: Perceptions vs. Reality." *Physics Today* 38 (June 1985), 34-45.

162   Rathjens, George. "The Strategic Defense Initiative: The Imperfections of 'Perfect Defense'." *Environment* 26 (June 1984), 6-13.

163   Rathjens, George and Jack Ruina. "BMD and Strategic Instability." *Daedalus* 114 (Summer 1985), 239-256.

164   Reed, Fred. "The Star Wars Swindle: Hawking Nuclear Snake Oil." *Harper's* 256 (May 1986), 39-48.

165   "Special Issue: Strategic Defense Initiative (SDI) Alias Star Wars." *F.A.S. Public Interest Report* 38 (Mar. 1985), 1-12.

166 Springer, John C. "Strategic Defense in Perspective: Nuclear Weapons and American Globalism." *Fletcher Forum* 10 (Winter 1986), 65-92.

167 Von Hippel, Frank. "Attacks on Star Wars Critics a Diversion." *Bulletin of the Atomic Scientists* 41 (Apr. 1985), 8-10.

SDI ADVOCATES

Gray (172-173) and Jastrow (175) are two of the most prolific and outspoken supporters of SDI. Graham (169) is certainly the most enthusiastic grass-roots supporter and his concept of the "High Frontier" closely approximates what many believe to be a design for an SDI early deployment.

Books

168 Gardner, John; Edward Gerry; Robert Jastrow; William Nierenberg; and Frederick Seitz. *Deployment of Missile Defense in the 1990s.* Washington, D.C.: George C. Marshall Institute, 1986. 2nd ed., Feb. 1987.

169 Graham, Lt. Gen. Daniel O. *High Frontier: A New National Strategy.* rev. ed. Washington, D.C.: Heritage Foundation, 1982.

170 Graham, Lt. Gen. Daniel O. *We Must Defend America—And Put an End to MADness.* Chicago: Regnery Gateway, 1983.

171 Graham, Lt. Gen. Daniel O. and Gregory A. Fossedale. *A Defense That Defends: Blocking Nuclear Attack.* Greenwich, CT: Dilvin-Adair, 1983.

172 Gray, Colin S. *American Military Space Policy: Information Systems, Weapons Systems and Arms Control.* Cambridge, MA: Abt Books, 1983. (vulnerability of U.S. satellites requires defenses in space as)

173 Gray, Colin S. *Nuclear Strategy and National Style.* Lanham, MD: Hamilton, 1986.

174 Hoffman, Fred S. *1983 Summary Report: Ballistic Missile Defenses and U.S. National Security.* Washington, D.C.: Institute for Defense Analysis, Oct. 1983. (so-called Hoffman report)

175 Jastrow, Robert. *How to Make Nuclear Weapons Obsolete.* Boston: Little, Brown, 1985.

176 Keyworth, George A. *Security and Stability: the Role for Strategic Defense.* San Diego, CA: Institute on Global Conflict and Cooperation, University of California, San Diego, 1985. (Science advisor to President Reagan)

177 Larson, Joyce E. and William C. Brodie. *The Intelligent Layperson's Guide to "Star Wars": 16 Questions and Answers on Strategic Defense*

and Space Weaponry. New York: National Strategy Information Center, 1986.

178   Payne, Keith B. *Strategic Defense: "Star Wars" in Perspective.* Lanham, MD: Hamilton Press, 1986.

179   Department of State. *The Strategic Defense Initiative.* Special Report No. 129. Washington, D.C.: Bureau of Public Affairs, June 1985.

180   Weinrod, W. Bruce, ed. *Assessing Strategic Defense: Six Roundtable Discussions.* Washington, D.C.: Heritage Foundation, 1985.

Articles

181   Abrahamson, Lt. Gen. James A. "Abrahamson cites potential of ground-based laser defense." *Aviation Week & Space Technology* 123 (Oct. 14, 1985), 22-23. (Director of SDIO)

182   Abrahamson, Lt. Gen. James A. "The SDI: Programme and Rationale." *Survival* 27 (March/April 1985), 75-78. (provides schedule for SDI)

183   Abrahamson, Lt. Gen. James A. "The Strategic Defense Initiative." *Defense/84* (Aug. 1984), 3-11.

184   Adelman, Kenneth L. *SDI: Setting the Record Straight.* Current Policy No. 730. Washington, D.C.: U.S. Department of State, Bureau of Public Affairs, Aug. 1985.

185   Dale, Reginald. "The Case for Star WArs." *Atlantic Community Quarterly* 23 (Fall 1985), 229-232.

186   Gliksman, Alex. "Strategic Defense Business: An Interview with Lt. Gen. James Abrahamson." *National Defense* 71 (Mar. 1986), 52-58.

187   Graham, Lt. Gen. Daniel O. "It's Time for High Frontier." *Journal of Social, Political and Economic Studies* 9 (Summer 1984), 180-183.

188   Gray, Colin S. "A Case for Strategic Defense." *Survival* 27 (Mar./Apr. 1985), 50-54.

189   Gray, Colin S. "The Transition from Offense to Defense." *Washington Quarterly* 9 (Summer 1986), 59-72.

190   Greenley, Brendon M., Jr. "SDIO Stresses Gains in ICBM Intercept." *Aviation Week & Space Technology* 123 (May 19, 1986), 24-25.

191   Jastrow, Robert. "Reagan vs. the Scientists: Why the President is Right About Missile Defense." *Commentary* 77 (Jan. 1984), 23-32.

192   Keyworth, George A., II. "The Case for Strategic Defense: An Option for a World Disarmed." *Issues in Science and Technology* 1 (Fall 1984), 30-44.

193   Keyworth, George A., II. "A Sense of Obligation: the Strategic Defense Initiative." *Aerospace America* 22 (Apr. 1984), 56-62.

194 Lawyer, John E. "Beyond Deterrence: The Strategic Defense Option." *Air University Review* 36 (Nov./Dec. 1984), 32-41.

195 Lebow, Richard Ned. "If I Were Reagan: Stopping the Arms Race." *SAIS Review* 5 (Summer-Fall 1985), 125-132.

196 Lehrman, Lewis E. "The Case for Strategic Defense." *Policy Review* 31 (Winter 1985), 42-49.

197 McFarlane, Robert C. *Strategic Defense Initiative.* Current Policy No. 670. Washington, D.C.: U.S. Department of State, Bureau of Public Affairs, Mar. 7, 1985.

198 Nitze, Paul H. *The Promise of SDI.* Washington, D.C.: U.S. Department of State, Bureau of Public Affairs, Mar. 1986.

199 Nitze, Paul H. "SDI: Its Nature and Rationale." *Atlantic Community Quarterly* 23 (Fall 1985), 263-268. (also printed as U.S. Department of State, Current Policy no. 751.

200 Payne, Keith B. "Strategic Defense and Stability." *Orbis* 28 (Summer 1984), 215-226.

201 Perle, Richard N. "The Strategic Defense Initiative: Addressing Some Misconceptions." *Journal of International Affairs* 39 (Summer 1985), 23-30.

202 Robinson, Clarence A., Jr. "Why Strategic Defense Criticism is Obsolete." *Policy Review* 37 (Summer 1986), 16-23.

203 "SDI: Will We Be More Secure in 2010?" A Forum with Albert Gore, Jr., Paul H. Nitze, Franz-Joseph Schulze, Robert W. Komer, Eugen V. Rostow. *Atlantic Community Quarterly* 24 (Fall 1986), 179-218.

204 Snow, Donale M. "BMD, SDI, and Future Policy: Issues and Prospectives." *Air University Review* 36 (July/Aug. 1985), 4-13.

205 Teller, Edward. "Science and Technology in the Strategic Defense Initiative." *Defense Science 2003+* 4 (Apr./May 1985), 17-24.

206 Toomay, John C. "The Case for Ballistic Missile Defense." *Daedalus* 114 (Summer 1985), 219-238. (member of the "Fletcher" panel)

207 Weinberger, Caspar W. "U.S. Defense Strategy." *Foreign Affairs* 64 (Spring 1986), 675-697.

208 Windmiller, David E. "SDI: A Strategy for Peace and Stability or the End to Deterrence?" *Parameters: Journal of the U.S. Army War College* 16 (Summer 1986), 16-25.

209 Yonas, Gerold. "The Strategic Defense Initiative." *Daedalus* 114 (Spring 1985), 73-90.

210 Yonas, Gerold. "Strategic Defense Initiative: The Politics and Science of Weapons in Space." *Physics Today* 38 (June 1985), 24-32.

SOVIETS AND SDI

The Soviet Union has vehemently opposed Reagan's SDI plan; Holloway (214), Garthoff (211) and a report by Soviet scientists (221) review their position. Van Cleave (224) argues that Reagan's SDI program is a justified response to one under way in the U.S.S.R.; while Stevens (222) and Rivkin (219) suggest that the Soviet outcry is less than sincere.

211 Garthoff, Raymond L. "BMD and East-West Relations." In Ashton B. Carter and David N. Schwartz, eds. *Ballistic Missile Defense.* Washington, D.C.: Brookings, 1984, pp. 275-329.

212 Goure, Daniel. "Soviet Counters to SDI." *NATO's Sixteen Nations* 31 (Apr. 1986), 34-37.

213 Haslam, Jonathan. "The Soviet Union and the Strategic Defense Initiative: Problems and Prospects." In Simon Serfaty, ed. *U.S.-Soviet Relations.* Washington, D.C.: Foreign Policy Institute School of Advanced Studies, Johns Hopkins University, Aug. 1985, pp. 33-38.

214 Hollaway, David. "The Strategic Defense Initiative and the Soviet Union." *Daedalus* 114 (Summer 1985), 257-278.

215 Krebs, Thomas H. "Ballistic Missile Defense: Soviet Countermeasures." *Defense Science 2003+* 4 (Aug./Sept. 1985), 65-75.

216 Meyer, Stephen M. "Soviet Views on SDI." *Survival* 27 (Nov./Dec. 1985), 274-292.

217 Nitze, Paul H. *The Impact of SDI on U.S.-Soviet Relations.* Current Policy No. 830. Washington, D.C.: U.S. Department of State, Bureau of Public Affairs, 1986.

218 Payne, Keith B. "The Soviet Union and Strategic Defense: The Failure and Future of Arms Control." *Orbis* 29 (Winter 1986), 673-688.

219 Rivkin, David B., Jr. "What Does Moscow Think?" *Foreign Policy* no. 59 (Summer 1985), 85-105. (reviews various views)

220 Shenfield, Stehphen. "Soviets May Not Imitate Star Wars." *Bulletin of the Atomic Scientists* 41 (June/July 1985), 38-39.

221 "Space-Based Defenses: A Soviet Study Report by Committee of Soviet Scientists, Institute of Space Research, U.S.S.R. Academy of Sciences, 1984." *Survival* 27:2 (Mar./Apr. 1985), 83-89.

222 Stevens, Sayre. "The Soviet Factor in SDI." *Orbis* 29:4 (Winter 1986), 689-700.

223 Arms Control & Disarmament Agency. *The Soviet Propaganda Campaign Against the U.S. Strategic Defense Initiative.* ACDA No. 122. Washington, D.C.: U.S. ACDA, Aug. 1986.

224   Van Cleave, William R. *Fortress USSR: The Soviet Defense Initiative and the U.S. Strategic Defense Response.* Stanford, CA: Hoover Institution Press, 1986. (very pro-SDI)

U.S.-U.S.S.R COMPARISONS

225   Garwin, Richard, and John Pike. "Space Weapons." *Bulletin of the Atomic Scientists* 40 (May 1984), 48-49. (summarizes U.S.-U.S.S.R. BMD and ASAT)

226   Smith, Gerard C. "Star Wars is Still the Problem." *Arms Control Today* 116 (Mar. 1986), 3-6. (assessment of U.S.-U.S.S.R. capabilities)

227   Stares, Paul. "U.S. and Soviet Military Space Programs: A Comparative Assessment." *Daedalus* 114 (Spring 1985), 127-146.

228   Stares, Paul B. *Space and National Security.* Washington, D.C.: Brookings Institution, 1987. (esp. ASAT programs)

229   Department of Defense. *Soviet Military Power.* Washington, D.C.: G.P.O., 1984, 1985, 1986.

SOVIET SDI CAPABILITIES

Much of the U.S.'s information about Soviet SDI capabilities is for obvious reasons classified. However, the joint Department of Defense and State Department report (246) on Soviet Strategic Defense Programs is a comprehensive appraisal. Stubb's assessement (245) of Soviet BMD efforts is one of the best unclassified works.

230   Davis, Jacquelyn K., *et al. The Soviet Union and Ballistic Missile Defense.* Cambridge, MA: Institute for Foreign Policy Analysis, 1980.

231   Davis, William A., Jr. *Asymmetries in U.S. and Soviet Strategic Defense Programs: Implications for Near-Term American Deployment Options.* Washington, D.C.: Policy Analysis, 1986.

232   Goure, Daniel and Gordon H. McCormick. "Soviet Strategic Defense: The Neglected Dimension of the U.S.-Soviet Balance." *Orbis* 24 (Spring 1980), 103-128. (strategic defense a substitute for offensive superiority)

233   Krebs, Thomas H. "The Soviet Space Threat." *Journal of Social, Political and Economic Studies* 9 (Summer 1984), 144-163.

234   Krepon, Michael and D. Geoffrey Peck. "Another Alarm on Soviet ABMs." *Bulletin of the Atomic Scientists* 41 (June/July 1985), 34-37.

235   Linn, Thomas C. "Soviet Strategic Initiative." *Defense and Foreign Affairs* 14 (Dec. 1986), 17-20.

236   Lord, Carnes. "Taking Soviet Defense Seriously." *Washington Quarterly* 9 (Fall 1986), 83-100.

237   Meyer, Stephen M. "Soviet Military Programs and the 'New High Ground'." *Survival* 25:5 (1983), 204-215.

238   Nitze, Paul H. *SDI: The Soviet Program.* Current Policy no. 717. Washington, D.C.: U.S. Department of State, Bureau of Public Affairs, 1985.

239   Richelson, Jeffrey T. "U.S. Intelligence and Soviet Star Wars." *Bulletin of the Atomic Scientists* 42 (May 1986), 12-14.

240   Rivkin, David B., Jr. and Manfred R. Hamm. *In Strategic Defense, Moscow is Ahead.* Washington, D.C.: Heritage Foundation, 1985.

241   Ruhle, Hans. "Gorbachev's 'Star Wars'." *Atlantic Community Quarterly* 23 (Winter 1985-86), 307-314.

242   Stevens, Sayre. "Ballistic Missile Defense in the Soviet Union." *Current History* 84 (Oct. 1985), 313-316.

243   Stevens, Sayre. "The Soviet BMD Program." In Ashton B. Carter and David N. Schwartz, eds. *Ballistic Missile Defense.* Washington, D.C.: Brookings, 1984, pp. 182-220.

244   Stubbs, Eric. "Soviet Strategic Defense Technology." *Bulletin of the Atomic Scientists* 43 (Spr. 1987), 14-19.

245   Stubbs, Eric. *Star Wars: The Soviet Program.* New York: Council on Economic Priorities Report, 1986.

246   Department of Defense, Department of State. *Soviet Strategic Defense Programs.* Washington, D.C.: G.P.O., Oct. 1985.

SOVIET MILITARY STRATEGY & SDI

247   Deane, Michael J. *The Role of Strategic Defense and Soviet Strategy.* Coral Gables, FL: Advanced International Studies Institute in Association with the University of Miami, 1980.

248   Kupperman, Robert H. "Using SDI to Reshape Soviet Strategic Behavior." *Washington Quarterly* 8 (Summer 1985), 77-84.

249   Linville, Ray P. "Emerging Soviet Space Systems: Prospects for Military Application." *Armed Forces Journal International* 124 (Jan. 1987), 32-35.

250   McConnell, James M. "Shifts in Soviet Views on the Proper Focus of Military Development." *World Politics* 37 (Apr. 1985), 317-343.

251   Roberts, Cynthia A. "Soviet Military Policy in Transition." *Current History* 83 (Oct. 1984), 331-346.

RELATED SOVIET TECHNOLOGY

Aviation Week & Space Technology is prompt in reporting suspected Soviet technological achievements related to BMD.

252 Beam, Alexander. "Russia Gropes for a Way to Enter the High Tech Age." *Business Week* (Nov. 11, 1985), 98-102.

253 Canby, Thomas Y. "Are the Soviets Ahead in Space?" *National Geographic* 170 (Oct. 1986), 420-459.

254 Goodman, Seymour E. "Soviet Computing and Technology Transfer: An Overview." *Comparative Politics* 11 (July 1979), 539-570.

255 Pollack, M. and R.A. Stapleton. "Why Ivan Can't Compute." *High Technology* (Feb. 1986), 42-45.

256 Robinson, Clarence A., Jr. "Soviets Build Directed-Energy Weapon." *Aviation Week & Space Technology* 117 (July 28, 1980), 47-50.

257 Robinson, Clarence A., Jr. "Soviets Test Beam Technologies in Space." *Aviation Week & Space Technology* 115 (Nov. 13, 1978), 14-20.

258 Snell, Paul. "Soviet Microprocessors and Microcomputers." In Ronald Amann and Julian Cooper, eds. *Technical Progress and Soviet Economic Development*. Oxford: Basil Blackwell, 1986, pp. 51-74.

SOVIET CRITICISM OF U.S.'S SDI

Listed here is a sampling of Moscow's critical comments.

259 Israelyan, V. "U.S.A. Torpedoes Disarmament." *International Affairs (USSR)* 11 (Nov. 1984), 46-54.

260 Kozyrev, A. "For Peaceful Outer Space." *International Affairs (USSR)* 5 (May 1985), 122-129.

261 Kuznetsova, I. and Yu. Orlov. "U.S.A.'s Dangerous Undertakings in Outer Space." *International Affairs (USSR)* 12 (Dec. 1985), 116-121.

262 Menshikov, S. "What is Behind the 'Star Wars' Debate?" *International Affairs (USSR)* 6 (June 1985), 67-77.

263 Ovinnikov, R. "'Star Wars' Programme - A New Phase in Washington's Milatiristic Policy." *International Affairs (USSR)* 8 (Aug. 1985), 13-22.

264 Piradov, A. "To Prevent Militarization of Outer Space." *International Affairs (USSR)* 9 (Sept. 1984), 93-96.

265 Platonov, A. "Militarization of Outer Space - A Threat to Mankind." *International Affairs (USSR)* 2 (Feb. 1985), 28-36.

266 Somov, M. "'Star Peace,' Not 'Star Wars'." *International Affairs (USSR)* 3 (Mar. 1986), 54-62.

267 Tomilin, Y. "To Avert the Threat of Militarizing Outer Space." *International Affairs (USSR)* 6 (June 1984), 61-67.

268 Velikhov, Y. "Space Ambitions - Earthly Threats." *International Affairs (USSR)* 7 (July 1984), 62-65.

EUROPE AND SDI

A discussion of SDI and Europe revolves essentially around alliance (NATO) politics. Presented initially are the more general reviews of issues and attitudes.

269 Brauch, Hans G. *From "Star Wars" to Strategic Defense Initiative: European Perceptions and Assessments.* New York: St. Martin's, 1986.

270 Daalder, Ivo H. *The SDI Challenge to Europe.* Cambridge, MA: Ballinger, 1987.

271 Hamm, Manfred R. and W. Bruce Weinrod. "The Transatlantic Politics of Strategic Defense." *Orbis* 29 (Winter 1986), 709-734. (pro-SDI)

272 Holm, Hans-Henrik. "SDI and European Security: Does Dependence Assume Security?" *Alternatives: A Journal of World Policy* 10:4 (1985), 517-532.

273 Kennet, Wayland. "Star Wars: Europe's Polite Waffle." *Bulletin of the Atomic Scientists* 41 (Sept. 1985), 7-11.

274 Koehl, Stuart. "The Strategic Defense Initiative and Its Potential for European Industry." *Journal of Social, Political and Economic Studies* 10 (Winter 1985), 387-406.

275 Kozicharow, E. "SDI Organization Moves to Promote Non-U.S. Share of Research Work." *Aviation Week & Space Technology* 122 (Apr. 29, 1985), 215-221.

276 Lucas, Michael. "Militarizaton or Common Security?" *World Policy Journal* 3 (Winter 1985-86), 219-250.

277 Lucas, Michael. "SDI and Europe." *World Policy Journal* 3 (Spring 1986), 219-249.

278 Menaul, Stewart. "Europe's Stake in Ballistic Missile Defense." *Journal of Social, Political and Economic Studies* 9 (Summer 1984), 184-195.

279 Seitz, Konrad. "SDI: The Technological Challenge for Europe." *World Today* 41: (Aug./Sept. 1985), 154-157.

280 White, Andrew. "European Perspectives on the Strategic Defense Initiative." *Millenium: Journal of International Studies* 15 (Summer 1986), 211-222.

281   Wilkinson, John and T.B. Millar, Marie-France Garaud. "Foreign Perspectives on the SDI." *Daedalus* 114 (Summer 1985), 297-314.

282   Yost, David S. "European Anxieties About Ballistic Missile Defense." *Washington Quarterly* 7 (Fall 1984), 112-129.

NATO AND SDI

Reagan's SDI proposal has put increased strains on the NATO alliance, which is concerned about removing the U.S. nuclear umbrella. Lellouche (295) is critical of SDI; while Sorenson (299) examines the theater applications of BMD. Gallis, Lowenthal and Smith (290) survey European concerns.

283   Bertram, Christopher. "Strategic Defense and the Western Alliance." *Daedalus* 114 (Summer 1985), 279-296.

284   Bertram, Christopher. "Strategic Defense in Europe." *NATO's Sixteen Nations* 31 (June 1986), 28-32.

285   Bluth, Christopher. "SDI: The Challenge to West Germany." *International Affairs* (Great Britain) 62 (Spring 1986), 247-264.

286   DeSantis, Hugh. "SDI and the European Allies: Riding the Tiger." *Arms Control Today* 16 (Mar. 1986), 7-10.

287   Dean, Jonathan. "Will NATO Survive Ballistic Missile Defense?" *Journal of International Affairs* 39 (Summer 1985), 95-114.

288   Fenske, John. "France and the Strategic Defense Initiative: Speeding Up or Putting on the Brakes?" *International Affairs* (Great Britain) 62 (Spring 1986), 231-246.

289   Froman, Michael B., et al. "France and SDI." *Naval War College Review* 40 (spring 1987), 37-43.

290   Gallis, Paul E., Mark M. Lowenthal and Marcia S. Smith. *The Strategic Defense Initiative and United States Alliance Strategy.* Report No. 85-48-F. Washington, D.C.: Congressional Research Service, Feb. 1, 1985.

291   Geneste, Marc. "Strategic Defense and the Shield of Europe." *Atlantic Community Quarterly* 23 (Summer 1985), 157-164.

292   Kanter, Arnold. "Thinking About the Strategic Defense Initiative: An Alliance Perspective." *International Affairs* (Great Britain) 61 (Summer 1985), 449-464.

293   Hiebert, Timothy H. "Reagan's Strategic Defense Initiative: The U.S. Presentation and the European Response." *Fletcher Forum* 10:1 (Winter 1986), 51-64.

294 Lellouche, Pierre. "SDI and the Atlantic Alliance." *SAIS Review* 5 (Summer-Fall 1985), 67-80. (critical of SDI)

295 Lellouche, Pierre. "SDI and the Atlantic Alliance." *Atlantic Community Quarterly* 23 (Fall 1985), 211-222.

296 Nerlich, Uwe. "Missile Defences: Strategic and Tactical." *Survival* 27 (May/June 1985), 119-127.

297 Rowny, Edward. "SDI and Europe." *NATO: Sixteen Nations* 30 (Dec. 1985/Jan. 1986), 43-44.

298 Schulze, Franz-Joseph. "SDI and the Conventional Defense of Europe." *International Defense Review* no. 9 (1986), 1225-1232.

299 Sorenson, David S. "Ballistic Missile Defense for Europe." *Comparative Strategy* 5:2 (1985), 159-178. (theater applications of BMD)

300 Taylor, Trevor. "Britain's Response to the Strategic Defense Initiative." *International Affairs* (Great Britain) 62 (Spring 1986), 217-230.

301 Weinberger, Caspar. "Letter to the Allies on SDI Research, March 26, 1985." *Survival* 27 (May/June 1985), 128.

302 Wells, Samuel F. "The United States and European Defense Cooperation." *Survival* 27 (July/Aug. 1985), 158-168.

303 Yost, David S. "Soviet Ballistic Missile Defense and NATO." *Orbis* 29 (Summer 1985), 281-292.

OTHER NATIONS AND SDI

Other nations have reacted strongly to SDI; the following is a sampling of views from Canada and Asia.

304 Clugston, M. "A Polite 'No' to Star Wars." *MacLeans* 98 (Sept. 16, 1985), 10-11. (Canadian Government)

305 Glaser, Bonnie S. and Banning N. Garrett. "Chinese Perspectives on the Strategic Defense Initiative." *Problems of Communism* 35 (Mar./Apr. 1986), 28-44.

306 Holmes, Kim R. "U.S.-Soviet-China Relations and Strategic Defense." Washington, D.C.: Heritage Foundation, 1986.

307 Mueller, David. "Inescapable SDI." *International Perspectives* (Canada). (Sept./Oct. 1986), 14-16.

308 Petrov, D. "Japan and Space Militarization Plans." *International Affairs (USSR)* 6 (June 1986), 56-64.

309 Rohrlich, Paul E. "Canada and Star Wars." *International Perspectives* (May/June 1985), 17-20.

310 Ross, Douglas A. *Coping with "Star Wars": Issues for Canada and the Alliance.* Aurora Papers #2. Ottawa: Canadian Center for Arms Control and Disarmament, 1985.

311 Takase, Shojio. "What Star Wars Means to Japan." *Japan Quarterly* 32 (July/Sept. 1985), 240-247.

312 Wirick, Gregory. *Canadian Responses to the Strategic Defense Initiative.* Ottawa: Canadian Institute for International Peace & Security, 1985.

MILITARY ACTIVITIES IN SPACE

A general survey of activities can be found in Jasani (319). Gray (318) argues for a more active U.S. policy in space including the employment of different weapons systems.

313 Aftergood, Steven. "Nuclear Mishaps and Star Wars." *Bulletin of the Atomic Scientists* 42 (Oct. 1986), 40-44.

314 Andelman, David A. "Space Wars." *Foreign Policy* no. 44 (Fall 1981), 94-106.

315 Baker, David. *The Shape of Wars to Come.* Cambridge: Cambridgeshire, Stephens, 1981.

316 Bulkeley, Rip and Graham Spinardi. *Space Weapons: Deterrence or Delusion.* Totowa, NJ: Rowman & Littlefield, 1986.

317 Durch, William J., ed. *National Interests and the Military Use of Space.* Cambridge, MA: Ballinger, 1984.

318 Gray, Colin S. *America's Military Space Policy.* Cambridge, MA: Abt, 1982.

319 Jasani, Bhupendra. "Expansion of the Arms Race into Outer Space." *Bulletin of Peace Proposals* 17:3/4 (1986), 331-340.

320 Jasani, Bhupendra. *Outer Space: A New Dimension of the Arms Race.* London: Taylor & Francis, 1982.

321 Jasani, Bhupendra. *Space Weapons: The Arms Control Dilemma.* London: Taylor & Francis, 1984.

322 Jasani, Bhupendra and Christopher Lee. *Countdown to Space War.* London: Taylor & Francis, 1984.

323 Karas, Thomas H. *The New High Ground: Systems and Weapons of Space Age War.* New York: Simon & Schuster, 1983.

324 Manno, Jack. *Arming the Heavens: The Hidden Military Agenda for Space, 1945-1995.* New York: Dodd, Mead, 1984.

325 Mark, Hans. "War and Peace in Space." *Journal of International Affairs* 39 (Summer 1985), 1-22.

326 Macvey, John. *Space Weapons, Space War.* New York: Stein & Day, 1979.

327 Ritchie, David. *Spacewar.* New York: Atheneum, 1982.

328 Sewall, Sarah. "Militarizing the Last Frontier: The Space Weapons Race." *Defense Monitor* 12 (Nov. 5, 1983). Entire issue.

329 Stares, Paul B. *The Militarization of Space: U.S. Policy, 1945-1984.* New York: Cornell University Press, 1985.

330 Stine, G. Harry. *Confrontation in Space.* Englewood Cliffs, NJ: Prentice-Hall, 1981.

331 Zuckerman, Lord. *Star Wars in a Nuclear World.* London: Kimber, 1986. (deals with arms control & arms issues, including SDI)

ARMS CONTROL, DETERRENCE, STRATEGY & SDI

The SDI program could have a substantial impact on these other concepts. The books and articles listed here (only a sampling of available materials) are suggestive of the issues involved.

333 Dallmeyer, Dorinda G., ed. *The Strategic Defense Initiative: New Perspectives on Deterrence.* Boulder, CO: Westview, 1986.

334 Gray, Colin S. "Deterrence, Arms Control and the Defense Transition." *Orbis* 28 (Summer 1984), 227-239.

335 Kober, Stanley. "Strategic Defense, Deterrence, and Arms Control." *Washington Quarterly* 10 (Winter 1987), 123-135.

ARMS CONTROL AND SDI

Some of SDI's implications for arms control are discussed by Boutwell and Scribner (338) and DiMaggio (340); Schlesinger (354) argues for using SDI to negotiate a meaningful treaty on strategic weapons. See also *ABM Treaty*, below, for an immediate clash between SDI and arms control.

336 Adelman, Kenneth L. "Arms Control With and Without Agreements." *Foreign Affairs* 63 (Winter 1984), 240-263. (U.S. Arms Control and Disarmament chief)

337 *Arms Control and the Strategic Defense Initiative: Three Perspectives.* Occasional Paper 36. Muscatine, Iowa: Stanley Foundation, Oct. 1985.

338 Boutwell, Jeffrey and Richard A. Scribner. *The Strategic Initiative: Some Arms Control Implications.* Washington, D.C.: American Association for the Advancement of Science, May 1985.

339   Bundy, McGeorge and George F. Kennan, Robert S. McNamara, Gerard Smith. "The President's Choice: Star Wars or Arms Control." *Foreign Affairs* 63 (Winter 1984), 264-278.

340   DiMaggio, Cosmo. *The Effect of a Comprehensive Test Ban on the Strategic Defense Initiative.* Washington, D.C.: Congressional Research Service, Library of Congress, Oct. 1985.

341   Drell, Sidney D. "Star Wars and Arms Control." *Scientia* 120 (Oct. 1985), 383-393.

342   Freedman, Lawrence. "Star Wars and the Summit." *Government and Opposition* 21 (Spring 1986), 131-145.

343   Glynn, Patrick. "Star Wars and Arms Control: It's Not a Question of Pursuing One or the Other. We Can Have Both." *New Republic* 194 (June 2, 1986), 20-23.

344   Gray, Colin S. "Space Arms Control: A Skeptical View." *Air University Review* 36 (Nov./Dec. 1985), 73-86.

345   Harris, William R. "Arms Control Treaties: How Do They Restrain Soviet Strategic Defense Programs?" *Orbis* 29 (Winter 1986), 701-708.

346   Kampelman, Max M. "SDI and the Arms Control Process." *Atlantic Community Quarterly* 23 (Fall 1985), 223-228.

347   Keyworth, George A., II. "Strategic Defense: A Catalyst for Arms Reductions." In *Proceedings of the Third Annual Seminar of the Center for Law and National Security.* Charlottesville, VA: University of Virginia, June 23, 1984.

348   Keyworth, George A., II. "Strategic Defense Initiative: The Rational Route to Effective Nuclear Arms Control." *Government Executive* 16 (June 1984), 32-35.

349   Lall, Betty G., Rosy Nimroody, and Paul D. Brandes. *Security Without Star Wars: Verifying a Ban on Ballistic Missile Defense.* New York: Council on Economic Priorities, 1987.

350   Matsunaga, Spark M. "U.S.-Soviet Space Cooperation and Arms Control." *Bulletin of the Atomic Scientists* 41 (Mar. 1985), 17-21.

351   Nitze, Paul H. *SDI, Arms Control, and Stability: Toward a New Synthesis.* Current Policy No. 845. Washington, D.C.: U.S. Department of State, Bureau of Public Affairs, 1986.

352   Pfaltzgraff, Roert L. Jr. "Summitry, SDI, and Arms Control." *Fletcher Forum* 10 (Winter 1986), 39-42.

353   Pilat, Joseph. "Star Peace: Soviet Space Arms Control Strategy and Objectives." *Washington Quarterly* 10 (Winter 1987), 137-151.

354   Schlesinger, James R. "Rhetoric and Realities in the Star Wars Debate." *International Security* 10 (Summer 1985), 3-12. (sees SDI as a bargaining chip)

355 Schlesinger, James R. "SDI: The Quintessential Bargaining Chip." *Aerospace America* 23 (July 1985), 50-54.

356 Smith, Roger K. "The Separation of Arms Control Talks: The Reagan Redefinition of Arms Control and Strategy." *Millenium: Journal of International Studies* 15 (Summer 1986), 143-168.

357 Slocombe, Walter. "Arms Control and Strategic Defense: An Immediate Agenda for Arms Control." *Survival* 27 (Sept./Oct. 1985), 204-213.

358 U.S., House, Committee on Armed Services. The Defense Panel. Hearings; *The MX Missiles and the Strategic Defense Initiative: Their Implications on Arms Control Negotiations*. Washington, D.C.: G.P.O., 1985.

Anti-Satellite Treaty Prospects

SDI advocates oppose additional space arms control agreements such as an anti-satellite treaty (ASAT), see Covault (360) and Gray (362). Hafner (363) and Meyer (365) review the issues involved.

359 Bunn, George. "Open Skies for Missile Killers?" Arms Control Today 17:4 (1987), 14-17. (USSR may shoot down SDI space hardware)

360 Covault, Craig. "Soviet Antisatellite Treaty Raises Verification Issues." *Aviation Week & Space Technology* 120 (Aug. 29, 1983), 20-22.

361 Didisheim, Peter. *The ASAT/SDI Link: Papers on Strategic Defense.* Cambridge, MA: Union of Concerned Scientists, Winter/Spring 1986. (vulnerability of space-based defenses to ASAT attack)

362 Gray, Colin S. "Why an ASAT Treaty is a Bad Idea." *Aerospace America* 22 (Apr. 1984), 70-74. (space is already heavily militarized, so more is better)

363 Hafner, Donald L. "Averting a Brobdingnagian Skeet Shoot: Arms Control Measures for Anti-Satellite Weapons." *International Security* 5 (Winter 1980-81), 41-60. (suggests a treaty)

364 Langenberg, William H. "U.S. ASAT: Whither Now?" *Washington Quarterly* 9 (Fall 1986), 101-116.

365 Meyer, Stephen M. "Anti-Satellite Weapons and Arms Control: Incentives and Disincentives from the Soviet and American Perspectives." *International Journal* 36:3 (1981), 460-484.

366 Scheffran, Jurgen. "Verification and Risk for an Anti-Satellite Weapons Ban." *Bulletin of Peace Proposals* 17:2 (1986), 165-173.

367 Sigal, Leon V. "Antisatellite Accord Key to Summit." *Bulletin of the Atomic Scientists* 41 (Oct. 1985), 16-18.

368 Stares, Paul B. "Reagan and the ASAT Issue." *Journal of International Affairs* 39 (Summer 1985), 81-94.

DETERRENCE AND SDI

Since current deterrence strategies, such as mutual assured destruction and limited nuclear war, are much altered by the SDI program, a broad sampling of deterrence works are included here. For the novice and the informed, Wiesltier (381) and York (382) provide an understandable discussion of the role of deterrence.

369 Abshire, David M. "SDI: The Path to a More Mature Deterrent." *NATO Review* 33 (Apr. 1985), 8-16.

370 Berkowitz, Bruce D. "Prolifieration, Deterrence, and the Liklihood of Nuclear War." *Journal of Conflict Resolution* 29 (Mar. 1985), 112-136.

371 Gray, Colin S. "Strategic Defense, Deterrence, and the Prospects for Peace." *Ethics* 95 (Apr. 1985), 659-672. (pro-SDI)

372 Gormley, Dennis M. and Douglas M. Hart. "Soviet Views on Escalation." *Washington Quarterly* 7 (Fall 1984), 71-84.

373 Jervis, Robert; Richard Ned Lebow; and Janice Gross Stein. *Psychology and Deterrence.* Baltimore, MD: Johns Hopkins Press, 1985.

374 Kenny, Antony. *The Logic of Deterrence.* Chicago: University of Chicago Press, 1985.

375 Quester, George H. *The Future of Nuclear Deterrence.* Lexington, MA: Lexington Books, 1986.

376 Payne, Keith B. *Nuclear Deterrence in U.S.-Soviet Relations.* Boulder, CO: Westview, 1982.

377 Payne, Keith B. "The Deterrence Requirement for Defense." *Washington Quarterly* 9 (Winter 1986), 139-154.

378 Poole, Randall A. "Ballistic Missile Defense and Strategic Deterrence." *National Defense* 70 (Nov. 1985), 39-49.

379 Powell, Robert. "The Theoretical Foundation of Strategic Nuclear Deterrence." *Political Science Quarterly* 100 (Spring 1985), 75-96.

380 Sagdeev, Roald Z. and Oleg F. Prilutzkii. "Strategic Defense and Strategic Stability." *Scientia* 120 (Oct. 1985), 371-376.

381 Wiesltier, Leon. *Nuclear War, Nuclear Peace.* New York: Holt, Rhinehart & Winston, 1983. (an expanded version of his article in *The New Republic,* Jan. 10 & 17, 1983).

382 York, Herbert F. "Nuclear Deterrence and the Military Uses of Space." *Daedalus* 114 (Spring 1985), 17-32.

NUCLEAR STRATEGY, SYSTEMS AND SDI

Battlefield management, crucial for SDI, and its problems are reviewed by Bracken (384), Ford (385), and Ropelewski (397).

383   Betts, Richard K. "Compound Deterrence versus No-First-Use: What's Wrong Is What's Right." *Orbis* 28 (Winter 1985), 697-718.

384   Bracken, Paul. *The Command and Control of Nuclear Forces.* New Haven, CT: Yale University Press, 1983. (command and control is likely to falter in times of crisis)

385   Ford, Daniel. *The Button: The Pentagon's Strategic Command and Control System.* New York: Simon & Schuster, 1985.

386   Freedman, Lawrence. *The Evolution of Nuclear Strategy.* New York: St. Martin's, 1981.

387   Hardin, Russell; John J. Mearsheimer; Gerald Dworkin; and Robert E. Goodwin, eds. *Nuclear Deterrence, Ethics and Strategy.* Chicago: University of Chicago Press, 1986.

388   Hoffman, Fred S. "The SDI in U.S. Nuclear Strategy: Senate Testimony." *International Security* 10 (Summer 1985), 13-24.

389   Hunter, Robert E. "Pursuit for a U.S. Strategy Defense Endures." *Defense News* (Oct. 27, 1986), 19-20.

390   Hunter, Robert E. "SDI: Return to Basics." *Washingtin Quarterly* 9 (Winter 1986), 155-170.

391   Ikle, Fred C. "Nuclear Strategy: Can There Be a Happy Ending?" *Foreign Affairs* 63 (Spring 1985), 810-826.

392   Jervis, Robert. *The Illogic of American Nuclear Strategy.* Ithaca, NY: Cornell University Press, 1984.

393   McNamara, Robert. *Blundering Into Disaster: Surviving the First Century of the Nuclear Age.* New York: Pantheon, 1986.

394   McNamara, Robert S. and Hans A. Bethe. "Reducing the Risk of Nuclear War." *Atlantic Monthly* 256 (July 1985), 43-51. (No-First-Use)

395   Martel, William C. and Paul L. Savage. *Strategic Nuclear War: What the Superpowers Target and Why.* Westport, CT: Greenwood, 1986.

396   May, Michael M. "The U.S.-Soviet Approach to Nuclear Weapons." *International Security* 9 (Spring 1984), 140-153.

397   Ropelewski, Robert R. "Battle Management, C^3I Network Challenges Resources of SDI Office." *Aviation Week & Space Technology* 123 (July 15, 1985), 19-21.

398   Snow, Donald M. *Nuclear Strategy in a Dynamic World: American Policy in the 1980s.* University: University of Alabama Press, 1981.

ABM TREATY AND SDI

Several studies review the impact of SDI on the ABM Treaty, see especially, Drell, et al. (400), Longstreth, et al. (402), or Schneiter (407). Opponents of the ABM Treaty include the Heritage Foundation (409-410).

399 Bulkeley, Rip. *The Anti-Ballistic Missile Treaty, 1972-1983.* Peace Research Reports No. 3. Bradford, Eng.: School of Peace Studies, University of Bradford, Dec. 1983.

400 Drell, Sidney; Philip J. Farley and David Holloway. "Preserving the ABM Treaty: A Critique of the Reagan Strategic Defense Initiative." *International Security* 9 (Fall 1984), 51-91.

401 Gordon, Michael R. "Proposed U.S. Antisatellite System Threatens Arms Control in Space." *National Journal* 15 (Dec. 31, 1983), 2660-2665.

402 Longstreth, Thomas K. and John E. Pike. "U.S., Soviet Programs Threaten ABM Treaty." *Bulletin of the Atomic Scientists* 41 (Apr. 1985), 11-15.

403 Longstreth, Thomas K.; John E. Pike and John B. Rhinelander. *The Impact of U.S. and Soviet Ballistic Missile Defense Programs on the ABM Treaty.* 3rd. ed. Washington, D.C.: National Campaign to Save the ABM Treaty, Mar. 1985.

404 Paine, Christopher. "The ABM Treaty: Looking for Loopholes." *Bulletin of the Atomic Scientists* 39 (Aug./Sept. 1983), 13-17.

405 Payne, Keith B. and Rebecca V. Strode. "Space-Based Laser BMD: Strategic Policy and the ABM Treaty." *International Security Review* 7 (Fall 1982), 269-288.

406 Rhinelander, John B. "U.S. and Soviet Ballistic Missile Defense Programs: Implications for the 1972 ABM Treaty." *Space Policy* 2 (May 1986), 138-152.

407 Schneiter, George R. "Implications of the Strategic Defense Initiative for the ABM Treaty." *Survival* 27 (Sept./Oct. 1985), 213-225. (treaty under stress)

408 Smith, R. Jeffrey. "Star Wars Tests and the ABM Treaty." *Science* 221 (July 5, 1985), 29-31.

409 "A Time to Revise the ABM Treaty." *National Security Record* (Heritage Foundation) No. 49 (Sept. 1982), 1-2. (early opponents)

410 *Soviet Arms Accords Are No Bar to Reagan's Strategic Defense Initiative.* Backgrounder no. 421. Washington, D.C.: Heritage Foundation, Apr. 4, 1985.

411 Weinrod, W. Bruce. "Strategic Defense and the ABM Treaty." *Washington Quarterly* 9 (Summer 1986), 73-88.

Reagan Administration's Interpretation

The administration's position is stated by Nitze (415) and Sofaer (422). Critics include Kennedy (413), Rhinelander (420), and Sherr (421). The House Foreign Affairs Committee hearings (424) records both views.

412   "Early Dismantlement of the ABM Treaty." *Arms Control Today* 17 (Mar. 1987), 3-5. (critical)

413   Kennedy, Kevin C. "Treaty Interpretation by the Executive Branch: The ABM Treaty and 'Star Wars' Testing and Development." *American Journal of International Law* 80 (Oct. 1986), 854-877.

414   Levin, Carl. "Administration Wrong on ABM Treaty." *Bulletin of the Atomic Scientists* 43 (Apr. 1987), 30-33.

415   Nitze, Paul H. *SDI and the ABM Treaty.* Current Policy No. 711. Washington, D.C.: Department of State, Bureau of Public Affairs, June 1985. (also appears in U.S. Department of State *Bulletin* 85 (Aug. 1985), 37-39)

416   [Nunn, Sam.] "ABM Reinterpretation 'Fundamentally Flawed'." *Arms Control Today* 17 (Apr. 1987), 8-14, 38. (excerpts from Senator Nunn's Mar. 11, 12 &13, 1987 speechs)

417   Nunn, Sam. "Access to the ABM Treaty Record: The Senate's Constitutional Right." *Arms Control Today* 16 (Sept. 1986), 3-7.

418   Oberdorfer, Don. "ABM Reinterpretation: A Quick Study Young Lawyer's New Look at 1972 Pact Triggers Controversy." *Washington Post,* Oct. 22, 1986.

419   Rhinelander, John B. "How to Save the ABM Treaty." *Arms Control Today* 15 (May 1985), 1, 5-8.

420   Rhinelander, John B. "Reagan's Exotic Interpretation of the ABM Treaty: Legally, Historically, and Factually Wrong." *Arms Control Today* 15 (Oct. 1985), 3-6.

421   Sherr, Alan B. "Sound Legal Reasoning or Policy Expedient? The 'New Interpretation' of the ABM Treaty." *International Security* 11 (Winter 1986-1987), 71-93.

422   Sofaer, Abraham D. "The ABM Treaty and the Strategic Defense Initiative." *Harvard Law Review* 99 (May 1986), 1972-1985. (administration's position on ABM treaty)

423   Department of State. *The ABM Treaty and the SDI Program.* Current Policy Paper no. 755. Washington, D.C.: Bureau of Public Affairs, Oct. 1985. (Nitze & Sofaer defend administration)

424 House. Committee on Foreign Affairs. International Security and Science Subcommittee. Hearings; *ABM Treaty Interpretation Dispute.* Washington, D.C.: G.P.O., Oct. 22, 1985.

ABM Treaty Violations

In an effort to discredit the arms control process and justify its positions the administration (435) has accused the Soviets of violating various agreements, especially the ABM Treaty (434). Rebuttals to the administration's views include Bunn and Gellner (427), Pike (431), Schear (433).

425 Arkin, William M. "Long on Data, Short on Intelligence." *Bulletin of the Atomic Scientists* 43 (June 1987), 5-6. (questions Soviet violations)

426 "Arms Control Violations: The 1985 Report." *National Security Review* (Heritage Foundation) no. 77 (Mar. 1985), 1-6.

427 Bunn, M. Elaine and Charles R. Gellner. *Soviet Compliance with Arms Control Agreements (Excluding SALT I).* Washington, D.C.: Congressional Research Service, Library of Congress, May 24, 1978.

428 Burcharth, Martin. "Danes Bristle at U.S. Radar Plans." *Bulletin of the Atomic Scientists* 43 (June 1987), 11-13. (is Thule radar a U.S. violation?)

429 Cohen, Samuel and Joseph Douglass. "Arms Control, Verification and Deception." *National Security Review* (Heritage Foundation) no. 86 (Dec. 1985), 1-6.

430 Gordon, Michael. "CIA's Sceptical that new Soviet Radar Is Part of an ABM Defense System." *National Journal* 17 (Mar. 9, 1985), 765.

431 Pike, John E. and Jonathan Rick. "Charges of Treaty Violations; Much Less than Meets the Eye." *Federation of American Scientists Public Interest Report,* Mar. 1984.

432 Rubin, James P. "The Superpower Dispute Over Radars." *Bulletin of the Atomic Scientists* 43 (Apr. 1987), 34-37.

433 Schear, James A. "Arms Control Treaty Compliance: Buildup to a Breakdown?" *International Security* 10 (Fall 1985), 141-182. (reviews Reagan's accusation of Soviet "violations or probable violations" of the ABM and SALT II treaties)

434 Department of State. *Soviet Noncompliance With Arms Control Agreements.* Special Report no. 122. Washington, D.C.: Bureau of Public Affairs, Feb. 1, 1985.

435 Department of State. *U.S. Interim Restraint Policy: Responding to Soviet Arms Control Violations.* Special Report no. 147. Washington, D.C.: Bureau of Public Affairs, May 27, 1986.

436 Zimmerman, Peter. "The Thule, Fylingdales, and Krasnoyarsk Radars." *Arms Control Today* 17 (Mar. 1987), 9-11. (U.S. & U.S.S.R. have violated ABM treaty)

SDI TECHNOLOGY

Carter (442), Friel (445), OTA (447), and Zracket (448) review SDI systems. Jastrow (446) and Abrahamson (437) are more optimistic. For introduction to space weaponry, see Carter (442).

437 Abrahamson, James A. "The Strategic Defense Initiative: A Technical Summary." *NATO's Sixteen Nations* 31 (Apr. 1986), 38-41.

438 Bethe, Hans A., interviewed. "The Technology of Strategic Defense - Where We Stand and How Far We Can Go: An Interview with Hans A. Bethe." *Fletcher Forum* 10 (Winter 1986), 7-18.

439 Bethe, Hans A. and Jeffrey Boutwell, Richard L. Garwin. "BMD Technologies and Concepts in the 1980s." *Daedalus* 114 (Spring 1985), 53-72.

440 Bethe, Hans A. and Richard L. Garwin. "New BMD Technologies." *Daedalus* 114 (Summer 1985), Appendix A, 331-368.

441 Brown, Harold. "Is SDI Technically Feasible?" *Foreign Affairs* 64 (Apr. 1985), 435-454.

442 Carter, Ashton B. *Directed Energy Missile Defense In Space.* Office of Technology Assessment. Washington, D.C.: G.P.O., Apr. 1984.

443 Collins, Sean K. "Preferential Boost Phase Defense." *National Defense* 70 (Dec. 1985), 30-38.

444 Din, Allan W. "Strategic Defense Technology: Fact or Fiction?" *International Defense Review* 1:18 (1985), 29-34.

445 Friel, Patrick J. "U.S. Ballistic Missile Defense Technology: A Technical Overview." *Comparative Strategy* 4:4 (1984), 319-347.

446 Jastrow, Robert. "The Technical Feasibility of Ballistic Missile Defense." *Journal of International Affairs* 39 (Summer 1985), 45-56. "Technology in Space" issue.

447 Office of Technology Assessment. *Ballistic Missile Defense Technologies.* Washington, D.C.: G.P.O., Sept. 1985.

448 Zraket, Charles A. "Strategic Defense: A Systems Perspective." *Daedalus* 114 (Spring 1985), 109-126.

RELATED ISSUES

A sampling of the arguments about technology driving the arms race is presented here.

449 Archer, Dane. "University Management of Weapons Labs? No." *Bulletin of the Atomic Scientists* 42 (Jan. 1985), 41-44.

450 Berkowitz, Bruce D. "Technological Progress, Strategic Weapons, and American Nuclear Policy." *Orbis* 29 (Summer 1985), 241-258.

451 Bylinsky, Gene. "The High-Tech Race." *Fortune* 114 (Oct. 13, 1986), 28-38.

452 DeWitt, Hugh E. "Labs Drive the Arms Race." *Bulletin of the Atomic Scientists* 40 (Nov. 1984), 40-42.

453 Fischer, Dietrich. "Weapons Technology and the Intensity of Arms Races." *Conflict Management and Peace Science* 8 (Fall 1984), 49-70.

454 Kahn, James S. "University Management of Weapons Labs? Yes." *Bulletin of the Atomic Scientists* 42:1 (Jan. 1985), 39-40.

455 Lapp, Ralph E. *Arms Beyond Doubt: The Tyranny of Weapons Technology.* New York: Cowles, 1970.

456 Lewis, Kevin N. "Balance and Counterbalance: Technology and the Arms Race." *Orbis* 29 (Summer 1985), 259-267.

457 Rosen, Stephen. "Systems Analysis and the Quest for Rational Defense." *Public Interest* 76 (Summer 1984), 3-17.

SDI RESEARCH

458 Broad, William J. *Star Warriors: A Penetrating Look into the Lives of the Young Scientists Behind Our Space Age Weaponry.* New York: Simon & Schuster, 1985.

459 Brooks, Harvey, "The Strategic Defense Initiative as Science Policy." *International Security* 11 (Fall 1986), 177-184.

460 Foley, Theresa M. "SDI Organization Plans to Fund Theater Defense Architecture." *Aviation Week & Space Technology* 123 (May 19, 1986), 24-27. (contracts)

461 Friewald, David A. and Thomas E. Botts. "Wanted: Ground Simulator for SDI." *Aerospace America* 23 (July 1985), 80-81. (hardware)

462 Golden, Frederic. "Star Wars: The Research Heats Up." *Discover* 6 (Sept. 1985), 28-40.

463 Kim, Y.S.; H.S. Cho; and Z. Bien. "A New Guidance Law for Homing Missiles." *Journal of Guidance, Control, and Dynamics.* 8 (May-June 1985), 402-404. (engineering problems)

464 Rankine, Brig. Gen. Robert R., Jr. (USAF). "Research and Technology for Strategic Defense." *Aerospace America* 22 (Apr. 1984), 64-68, 80. (pro SDI)

465 Yonas, Gerald. "Research and the Strategic Defense Initiative." *International Security* 11 (Fall 1986), 185-189.

ANTI-SATELLITE SYSTEMS

The articles by Carter (466,467), Gottfried and Lebow (468), Manfredi (470), and May (471) outline the problems. Kane (469) is more optimistic. See also *Anti-Satellite Treaty Prospects*, above.

466 Carter, Ashton B. "The Relationship of ASAT and BMD Systems." *Daedalus* 114 (Spring 1985), 171-192.

467 Carter, Ashton B. "Satellites and Anti-Satellites: The Limits of the Possible." *International Security* 10 (Spring 1986), 46-98.

468 Gottfried, Kurt and Richard Ned Lebow. "Anti-Satellite Weapons: Weighing the Risks." *Daedalus* 114 (Spring 1985), 147-170.

469 Kane, Francis X. "Anti-Satellite Systems and U.S. Options." *Strategic Review* 10 (Winter 1982), 56-64.

470 Manfredi, Arthur F. *U.S. Military Satellites and Survivability.* Washington, D.C.: Congressional Research Service, Library of Congress, Feb. 1986.

471 May, Michael. "Safeguarding Our Military Space Systems." *Science* 222 (Apr. 18, 1986), 336-340.

472 Tirman, John. "Star Wars Technology Threatens Satellites." *Bulletin of the Atomic Scientists* 42 (May 1986), 28-32.

473 Union of Concerned Scientists. *Papers on Strategic Defense: Satellite Vulnerability.* Washington, D.C.: Union of Concerned Scientists, 1986.

474 Office of Technology Assessment. *Anti-Satellite Weapons, Countermeasures, and Arms Control.* Washington, D.C.: G.P.O., Sept. 1985.

LASERS, BEAMS & OTHER WEAPONS

Hecht (480) and DiMaggio (477) provide introductions to specific systems. The American Physical Society has published a comprehensive review of directed energy weapons (484). Also see Long, et al. (6).

475 Altmann, Jurgen. "Offensive Capabilities of Space-Based Lazers." *Bulletin of Peace Proposals* 17:2 (1986), 151-158.

476 Callahem, Michael and Kostas Tsipis. *High Energy Laser Weapons: A Technical Assessment.* Program in Science and Technology for International Security, Report #6. Cambridge, MA: MIT, Department of Physics, 1980. (highly technical evaluation of laser weapons for anti-satellite and anti-ballistic missile systems)

477 DiMaggio, Cosmo. *Directed Energy Weapons Research: Status and Outlook.* Washington, D.C.: Congressional Research Service, Library of Congress, Aug. 1985.

478 Dornheim, M.A. "Missile Destroyed in First SDI Test at High-Energy Laser Facility." *Aviation Week & Space Technology* 123 (Sept. 23, 1985), 17-19.

479 Fusion Energy Foundation Scientific Staff. *Beam Weapons: An Alternative to Nuclear Destruction.* Fallbrook, CA: Aero, 1984. (pro-SDI; explains various potential weapons)

480 Hecht, Jeff. *Beam Weapons: The Next Arms Race.* New York: Plenum, 1984.

481 Heppenheimer, T.A. "Zapping Missiles in Space." *High Technology* (Aug. 1985), 72-76.

482 Kaplan, Daniel. "Lasers for Missile Defense." *Bulletin of the Atomic Scientists* 39 (May 1983), 5-8.

483 Payne, Keith B. *Laser Weapons in Space.* Boulder, CO: Westview, 1983. "SDI Experiments Will Explore Viability of Ground-Based Laser." *Aviation Week & Space Technology* 123 (Aug. 18, 1986), 45-54.

484 *Report to The American Physical Society by the Study Group on Science and Technology of Directed Energy Weapons.* New York: The American Physical Society, Apr. 1987.

485 Smith, R. Jeffrey. "Experts Cast Doubts on X-Ray Laser, The Jewel of the Star Wars' Missile Defense Program Fails to Glitter." *Science* 230 (Nov. 8, 1985), 646-648. (skeptical)

486 Thompson, Barry L. "'Directed Energy' Weapons and the Strategic Balance." *Orbis* 23 (Fall 1979), 697-709.

COMPUTERS AND SOFTWARE

Parnas (494,495) is a prominent critic; Myers (491) surveys the debate.

487 The Eastport Study Group. *Computing in Support of Battle Management.* Washington, D.C.: DoD, Dec. 1985.

488 Jacky, Jonathan. "The 'Star Wars' Defense Won't Compute." *Atlantic Monthly* 255 (June 1985), 18-29.

489 Lin, Herbert. "The Development of Software for Ballistic Missile Defense." *Scientific American* 253 (Dec. 1985), 46-53.

490 Lin, Herbert. "The Software for Star Wars: An Achilles Heel?" *Technology Review* 88 (July 1985), 16-18.

491 Myers, Ware. "The Star Wars Software Debate." *Bulletin of the Atomic Scientists* 42 (Feb. 1986), 31-36.

492 Ornstein, Severo M. and Brian C. Smith, Lucy A. Suchman. "Strategic Computing." *Bulletin of the Atomic Scientists* 40 (Dec. 1984), 11-15.

493 "Panel Affirms Feasibility of Producing SDI Software." *Aviation Week & Space Technology* 123 (Dec. 9, 1985), 19.

494 Parnas, David Lorge. "Software Aspects of Strategic Defense Systems." *American Scientist* 73 (Sept./Oct. 1985), 432-440.

495 Parnas, David Lorge. "Software Aspects of Strategic Defense Systems." *SIGSOFT Software Engineering Notes* 10 (Oct. 1985), 15-23. (former member of SDIO's panel)

496 Parnas, David Lorge. "Why Star Wars Software Won't Work." *Harper's* 255 (Mar. 1985), 17-18.

497 Rose, Craig D. "SDI Won't Fly, Say Computer Experts. *Electronics* 58 (Oct. 28, 1985), 18-19.

Author Index
(Indexed by citation number)

Appendix A

The Conclusion of President Reagan's March 23, 1983, Speech on Defense Spending and Defensive Technology*

Now, thus far tonight I've shared with you my thoughts on the problems of national security we must face together. My predecessors in the Oval Office have appeared before you on other occasions to describe the threat posed by Soviet power and have proposed steps to address that threat. But since the advent of nuclear weapons, those steps have been increasingly directed toward deterrence of aggression through the promise of retaliation.

This approach to stability through offensive threat has worked. We and our allies have succeeded in preventing nuclear war for more than three decades. In recent months, however, my advisors, including in particular the Joint Chiefs of Staff, have underscored the necessity to break out of a future that relies solely on offensive retaliation for our security.

Over the course of these discussions, I've become more and more deeply convinced that the human spirit must be capable of rising above dealing with other nations and human beings by threatening their existence. Feeling this way, I believe we must thoroughly examine every opportunity for reducing tensions and for introducing greater stability into the strategic calculus on both sides.

One of the most important contributions we can make is, of course, to lower the level of all arms, and particularly nuclear arms. We're engaged right now in several negotiations with the Soviet Union to bring about a mutual reduction of weapons. I will report to you a week from tomorrow my thoughts on that score. But let me just say, I'm totally committed to this course.

If the Soviet Union will join with us in our effort to achieve major arms reduction, we will have succeeded in stabilizing the nuclear balance. Nevertheless, it will still be necessary to rely on the specter of retaliation, on mutual threat. And that's a sad commentary on the human condition. Wouldn't it be better to save lives than to avenge them? Are we not capable of demonstrating our peaceful intentions by applying all our abilities and our ingenuity to achieving a truly lasting stability? I think we are. Indeed, we must.

After careful consultation with my advisers, including the Joint Chiefs of Staffs, I believe there is a way. Let me share with you a vision of the future

*Weekly Compilation of Presidential Documents, 19:12, (March 28, 1983): 423-466.

which offers hope. It is that we embark on a program to counter the awesome Soviet missile threat with measures that are defensive. Let us turn to the very strengths in technology that spawned our great industrial base and that have given us the quality of life we enjoy today.

What if free people could live secure in the knowledge that their security did not rest upon the threat of instant U.S. retaliation to deter a Soviet attack, that we could intercept and destroy strategic ballistic missiles before they reached our own soil or that of our allies?

I know this is a formidable, technical task, one that may not be accomplished before the end of this century. Yet, current technology has attained a level of sophistication where it's reasonable for us to begin this effort. It will take years, probably decades of effort on many fronts. There will be failures and setbacks, just as there will be successes and breakthroughs. And as we proceed, we must remain constant in preserving the nuclear deterrent and maintaining a solid capability for flexible response. But isn't it worth every investment necessary to free the world from the threat of nuclear war? We know it is.

In the meantime, we will continue to pursue real reductions in nuclear arms, negotiating from a position of strength that can be ensured only by modernizing our strategic forces. At the same time, we must take steps to reduce the risk of a conventional military conflict escalating to nuclear war by improving our non-nuclear capabilities.

America does possess—now—the technologies to attain very significant improvements in the effectiveness of our conventional, non-nuclear forces. Proceeding boldly with these new technologies, we can significantly reduce any incentive that the Soviet Union may have to threaten attack against the United States or its allies.

As we pursue our goal of defensive technologies, we recognize that our allies rely upon our strategic offensive power to deter attacks against them. Their vital interests and ours are inextricably linked. Their safety and ours are one. And no change in technology can or will alter that reality. We must and shall continue to honor our commitments.

I clearly recognize that defensive systems have limitations and raise certain problems and ambiguities. If paired with offensive systems, they can be viewed as fostering an aggressive policy, and no one wants that. But with these considerations firmly in mind, I call upon the scientific community in our country, those who gave us nuclear weapons, to turn their great talents now to the cause of mankind and world peace, to give us the means of rendering these nuclear weapons impotent and obsolete.

Tonight, consistent with our obligations of the ABM treaty and recognizing the need for closer consultation with our allies, I'm taking an important first step. I am directing a comprehensive and intensive effort to define a long-term research and development program to begin to achieve our ultimate goal of eliminating the threat posed by strategic nuclear missiles. This could pave the way for arms control measures to eliminate the weapons themselves. We seek neither military superiority nor political advantage. Our only purpose—one all people share— is to search for ways to reduce the danger of nuclear war.

My fellow Americans, tonight we're launching an effort which holds the promise of changing the course of human history. There will be risks, and results take time. But I believe we can do it. As we cross this threshold, I ask for your prayers and your support.

Thank you, good night, and God bless you.

Appendix B

Texts of the 1972 ABM Treaty, Its Agreed Interpretations, and Its 1976 Protocol*

Treaty Between the United States of America and the Union of Soviet Socialist Republics on the Limitation of Anti-Ballistic Missile Systems

Signed at Moscow May 26, 1972
Ratification advised by U.S. Senate August 3, 1972
Ratified by U.S. President September 30, 1972
Proclaimed by U.S. President October 3, 1972
Instruments of ratification exchanged October 3, 1972
Entered into force October 3, 1972

The United States of America and the Union of Soviet Socialist Republics, hereinafter referred to as the Parties,

Proceeding from the premise that nuclear war would have devastating consequences for all mankind,

Considering that effective measures to limit anti-ballistic missile systems would be a substantial factor in curbing the race in strategic offensive arms and would lead to a decrease in the risk of outbreak of war involving nuclear weapons,

Proceeding from the premise that the limitation of anti-ballistic missile systems, as well as certain agreed measures with respect to the limitation of strategic offensive arms, would contribute to the creation of more favorable conditions for further negotiations on limiting strategic arms,

Mindful of their obligations under Article VI of the Treaty on the Non-Proliferation of Nuclear Weapons,

Declaring their intention to achieve at the earliest possible date the cessation of the nuclear arms race and to take effective measures toward reductions in strategic arms, nuclear disarmament, and general and complete disarmament,

Desiring to contribute to the relaxation of international tension and the strengthening of trust between states,

Have agreed as follows:

---

*US A.C.& D.A., *Arms Control and Disarmament Agreements: Texts and Histories of Negotiations*, Washington, D.C., 1982, 139-147 and 162-163.

Article I

1. Each party undertakes to limit anti-ballistic missile (ABM) systems and to adopt other measures in accordance with the provisions of this Treaty.

2. Each Party undertakes not to deploy ABM systems for a defense of the territory of its country and not to provide a base for such a defense, and not to deploy ABM systems for defense of an individual region except as provided for in Article III of this Treaty.

Article II

1. For the purpose of this Treaty an ABM system is a system to counter strategic ballistic missiles or their elements in flight trajectory, currently consisting of:

(a) ABM interceptor missiles, which are interceptor missiles constructed and deployed for an ABM role, or of a type tested in an ABM mode;

(b) ABM launchers, which are launchers constructed and deployed for launching ABM interceptor missiles; and

(c) ABM radars, which are radars constructed and deployed for an ABM role, of a type tested in an ABM mode.

2. The ABM system components listed in paragraph 1 of this Article include those which are:

(a) operational;

(b) under construction;

(c) undergoing testing;

(d) undergoing overhaul, repair or conversion; or

(e) mothballed.

Article III

Each Party undertakes not to deploy ABM systems or their components except that:

(a) within one ABM system deployment area having a radius of one hundred and fifty kilometers and centered on the Party's national capital, a Party may deploy: (1) no more than one hundred ABM launchers and no more than one hundred ABM interceptor missiles at launch sites, and (2) ABM radars within no more than six ABM radar complexes, the area of each complex being circular and having a diameter of no more than three kilometers; and

(b) within one ABM system deployment area having a radius of one hundred and fifty kilometers and containing ICBM silo launchers, a Party may deploy: (1) no more than one hundred ABM launchers and no more than one hundred ABM interceptor missiles at launch sites, (2) two large phased-array ABM radars comparable in potential to corresponding ABM radars operational or under construction on the date of signature of the Treaty in an ABM system deployment area containing ICBM silo launchers, and (3) no more than eighteen ABM radars each having a potential less than the potential of the smaller of the above-mentioned two large phased-array ABM radars.

Article IV

The limitations provided for in Article III shall not apply to ABM systems or their components used for development or testing, and located within current or additionally agreed test ranges. Each Party may have no more than a total of fifteen ABM launchers at test ranges.

Article V

1. Each Party undertakes not to develop, test, or deploy ABM systems or components which are sea-based, air-based, space-based, or mobile land-based.

2. Each Party undertakes not to develop, test, or deploy ABM launchers for launching more than one ABM interceptor missile at a time from each launcher, not to modify deployed launchers to provide them with such a capability, not to develop, test, or deploy automatic or semi-automatic or other similar systems for rapid reload of ABM launchers.

Article VI

To enhance assurance of the effectiveness of the limitations on ABM systems and their components provided by the Treaty, each Party undertakes:

(a) not to give missiles, launchers, or radars, other than ABM interceptor missiles, ABM launchers, or ABM radars, capabilities to counter strategic ballistic missiles or their elements in flight trajectory, and not to test them in an ABM mode; and

(b) not to deploy in the future radars for early warning of strategic ballistic missile attack except at locations along the periphery of its national territory and oriented outward.

Article VII

Subject to the provisions of this Treaty, modernization and replacement of ABM systems or their components may be carried out.

Article VIII

ABM systems or their components in excess of the numbers or outside the areas specified in this Treaty, as well as ABM systems or their components prohibited by this Treaty, shall be destroyed or dismantled under agreed procedures within the shortest possible agreed period of time.

Article IX

To assure the viability and effectiveness of this Treaty, each Party undertakes not to transfer to other States, and not to deploy outside its national territory, ABM systems or their components limited by this Treaty.

Article X

Each Party undertakes not to assume any international obligations which would conflict with this Treaty.

Article XI

The Parties undertake to continue active negotiations for limitations of strategic offensive arms.

Article XII

1. For the purpose of providing assurance of compliance with the provisions of this Treaty, each Party shall use national technical means of verification at its disposal in a manner consistent with generally recognized principles of international law.

2. Each Party undertakes not to interfere with the national technical means of verification of the other Party operating in accordance with paragraph 1 of this Article.

3. Each Party undertakes not to use deliberate concealment measures which impede verification by national technical means of compliance with the provisions of this Treaty. This obligation shall not require changes in current construction, assembly, conversion, or overhaul practices.

Article XIII

1. To promote the objectives and implementation of the provisions of this Treaty, the Parties shall establish promptly a Standing Consultative Commission, within the framework of which they will:

(a) consider questions concerning compliance with the obligations assumed and related situations which may be considered ambiguous;

(b) provide on a voluntary basis such information as either Party considers necessary to assure confidence in compliance with the obligations assumed;

(c) consider questions involving unintended interference with national technical means of verification;

(d) consider possible changes in the strategic situation which have a bearing on the provisions of this Treaty;

(e) agree upon procedures and dates for destruction or dismantling of ABM systems or their components in cases provided for by the provisions of this Treaty;

(f) consider, as appropriate, possible proposals for further increasing the viability of this Treaty; including proposals for amendments in accordance with the provisions of this Treaty;

(g) consider, as appropriate, proposals for further measures aimed at limiting strategic arms.

2. The Parties through consultation shall establish, and may amend as appropriate, Regulations for the Standing Consultative Commission governing procedures, composition and other relevant matters.

Article XIV

1. Each Party may propose amendments to this Treaty. Agreed amendments shall enter into force in accordance with the procedures governing the entry into force of this Treaty.

2. Five years after entry into force of this Treaty, and at five-year intervals thereafter, the Parties shall together conduct a review of this Treaty.

Article XV

1. This Treaty shall be of unlimited duration.

2. Each Party shall, in exercising its national sovereignty, have the right to withdraw from this Treaty if it decides that extraordinary events related to the subject matter of this Treaty have jeopardized its supreme interests. It shall give notice of its decision to the other Party six months prior to withdrawal from the Treaty. Such notice shall include a statement of the extraordinary events the notifying Party regards as having jeopardized its supreme interests.

Article XVI

1. This Treaty shall be subject to ratification in accordance with the constitutional procedures of each Party. The Treaty shall enter into force on the day of the exchange of instruments of ratification.

2. This Treaty shall be registered pursuant to Article 102 of the Charter of the United Nations.

DONE at Moscow on May 26, 1972, in two copies, each in the English and Russian languages, both texts being equally authentic.

FOR THE UNITED STATES OF AMERICA	FOR THE UNION OF SOVIET SOCIALIST REPUBLICS
RICHARD NIXON	**L.I. BREZHNEV**
President of the United States of America	General Secretary of the Central Committee of the CPSU

AGREED STATEMENTS, COMMON UNDERSTANDINGS, AND UNILATERAL STATEMENTS REGARDING THE TREATY BETWEEN THE UNITED STATES OF AMERICA AND THE UNION OF SOVIET SOCIALIST REPUBLICS ON THE LIMITATION OF ANTI-BALLISTIC MISSILES

1. Agreed Statements

The document set forth below was agreed upon and initialed by the heads of the Delegations on May 26, 1972 (letter designations added);

AGREED STATEMENTS REGARDING THE TREATY BETWEEN THE UNITED STATES OF AMERICA AND THE UNION OF SOVIET SOCIALIST REPUBLICS ON THE LIMITATION OF ANTI-BALLISTIC MISSILE SYSTEMS

[A]

The Parties understand that, in addition to the ABM radars which may be deployed in accordance with subparagraph (a) of Article III of the Treaty, those non-phased-array ABM radars operational on the date of signature of the Treaty within the ABM system deployment area for the defense of the national capital may be retained.

[B]

The Parties understand that the potential (the product of mean emitted power in watts and antenna area in square meters) of the smaller of the two large phased-array ABM radars referred to in subparagraph (b) of Article III of the Treaty is considered for purposes of the Treaty to be three million.

[C]

The Parties understand that the center of the ABM system deployment area centered on the national capital and the center of the ABM system deployment area containing ICBM silo launchers for each Party shall be separated by no less than thirteen hundred kilometers.

[D]

In order to insure fulfillment of the obligation not to deploy ABM systems and their components except as provided in Article III of the Treaty, the Parties agree that in the event ABM systems based on other physical principles and including components capable of substituting for ABM interceptor missiles, ABM launchers, or ABM radars are created in the future, specific limitations on such systems and their components would be subject to discussion in accordance with Article XIII and agreement in accordance with Article XIV of the Treaty.

[E]

The Parties understand that Article V of the Treaty includes obligations not to develop, test or deploy ABM interceptor missiles for the delivery by each ABM interceptor missile of more than one independently guided warhead.

[F]

The Parties agree not to deploy phased-array radars having a potential (the product of mean emitted power in watts and antenna area in square meters) exceeding three million, except as provided for in Articles III, IV, and VI of the Treaty, or except for the purposes of tracking objects in outer space or for use as national technical means of verification.

[G]

The Parties understand that Article IX of the Treaty includes the obligation of the U.S. and U.S.S.R. not to provide to other States technical descriptions or blue prints specially worked out for the construction of ABM systems and their components limited by the Treaty.

2. Common Understandings

Common understanding of the Parties on the following matters was reached during the negotiations:

A. Location of ICBM Defenses

The U.S. Delegation made the following statement on May 26, 1972:

Article III of the ABM Treaty provides for each side one ABM system deployment area centered on its national capital and one ABM system deployment area containing ICBM silo launchers. The two sides have registered agreement on the following statement: "The Parties understand that the center of the ABM system deployment area centered on the national capital and the center of the ABM system deployment area containing ICBM silo launchers for each party shall be separated by no less than thirteen hundred kilometers." In this connection, the U.S. side notes that its ABM system deployment area for defense of ICBM silo launchers, located west of the Mississippi River, will be centered in the Grand Forks ICBM silo launcher deployment area. (See Agreed Statement [C].)

B. ABM Test Ranges

The U.S. Delegation made the following statement on April 26, 1972:

Article IV of the ABM Treaty provides that "the limitations provided for in Article III shall not apply to ABM systems or their components used for development or testing, and located within current or additionally agreed test ranges." We believe it would be useful to assure that there is no misunderstanding as to current ABM test ranges. It is our understanding that ABM test ranges encompass the area within which ABM components are located for test purposes. The current U.S. ABM test ranges are at White Sands, New Mexico, and at Kwajalein Atoll, and the current Soviet ABM test range is near Sary Shagan in Kazakhstan. We consider that non-phased array radars of types used for range safety or instrumentation purposes may be located outside of ABM test ranges. We interpret the reference in Article IV to "additionally agreed test ranges" to mean that ABM components will not be located at any other test ranges without prior agreement between our Governments that there will be such additional ABM test ranges.

On May 5, 1972, the Soviet Delegation stated that there was a common understanding on what ABM test ranges were, that the use of the types of non-ABM radars for range safety or instrumentation was not limited under the treaty, that the reference in Article IV to "additionally agreed" test ranges was sufficiently clear, and that national means permitted identifying current test ranges.

C. Mobile ABM Systems
On January 29, 1972, the U.S. Delegation made the following statement:

Article V(1) of the Joint Draft Text of the ABM Treaty includes an undertaking not to develop, test, or deploy mobile land-based ABM systems and their components. On May 5, 1971, the U.S. side indicated that, in its view, a prohibition of deployment of mobile ABM systems and components would rule out the deployment of ABM launchers and radars which were not permanent fixed types. At that time, we asked for the Soviet view of this interpretation. Does the Soviet side agree with the U.S. side's interpretation put forward on May 5, 1971?

On April 13, 1972, the Soviet Delegation said there is a general common understanding on this matter.

D. Standing Consultative Commission
Ambassador Smith made the following statement on May 22, 1972:

The United States proposes that the sides agree that, with regard to initial implementation of the ABM Treaty's Article XIII on the Standing Consultative Commission (SCC) and of the consultation Articles to the Interim Agreement on offensive arms and the Accidents Agreement[1], agreement establishing the SCC will be worked out early in the follow-on SALT negotiations; until that is completed, the following arrangements will prevail: when SALT is in session, any consultation

---

[1]See Article 7 of Agreement to Reduce the Risk of Outbreak of Nuclear War Between the United States of America and the Union of Soviet Socialist Republics, signed Sept. 30, 1971, *ad hoc* arrangements for any desired consultations under these Articles may be made through diplomatic channels.

desired by either side under these Articles can be carried out by two SALT Delegations; when SALT is not in session, *ad hoc* arrangements for any desired consultations under these Articles may be made through diplomatic channels.

Minister Semenov replied that, on an *ad referendum* basis, he could agree that the U.S. statement corresponded to the Soviet understanding.

E. Standstill

On May 6, 1972, Minister Semenov made the following statement:

In an effort to accommodate the wishes of the U.S. side, the Soviet Delegation is prepared to proceed on the basis that the two sides will in fact observe the obligations of both the Interim Agreement and the ABM Treaty beginning from the date of signature of these two documents.

In reply, the U.S. Delegation made the following statement on May 20, 1972:

The U.S. agrees in principle with the Soviet statement made on May 6 concerning observance of obligations beginning from date of signature but we would like to make clear our understanding that this means that, pending ratification and acceptance, neither side would take any action prohibited by the agreements after they had entered into force. This understanding would continue to apply in the absence of notification by either signatory of its intention not to proceed with ratification or approval.

The Soviet Delegation indicated agreement with the U.S. statement.

3. Unilateral Statements

The following noteworthy unilateral statements were made during the negotiations by the United States Delegation:

A. Withdrawal from the ABM Treaty

On May 9, 1972, Ambassador Smith made the following statement:

The U.S. Delegation has stressed the importance the U.S. Government attaches to achieving agreement on more complete limitations on strategic offensive arms, following agreement on an ABM Treaty and on an Interim Agreement on certain measures with respect to the limitation of strategic offensive arms. The U.S. Delegation believes that an objective of the follow-on negotiations should be to constrain and reduce on a long-term basis threats to the survivability of our respective strategic retaliatory forces. The U.S.S.R. Delegation has also indicated that the objectives of SALT would remain unfulfilled without the achievement of an agreement providing for more complete limitations on strategic offensive arms. Both sides recognize that the initial agreements would be steps toward the achievement of more complete limitations on strategic arms. If an agreement providing for more complete strategic offensive arms limitations were not achieved within five years U.S. supreme interests could be jeopardized. Should that occur, it would constitute a basis for withdrawal from the ABM Treaty. The U.S. does not wish to see such a situation occur, nor do we believe that the U.S.S.R. does. It is because we wish to prevent such a situation that we emphasize the importance the U.S. Government attaches to achievement of more complete limitations on strategic offensive arms. The U.S. Executive will inform the Congress, in connection with Congressional consideration of the ABM Treaty and the Interim Agreement, of this statement of the U.S. position.

B. Tested in ABM Mode

On April 7, 1972, the U.S. Delegation made the following statement:

Article II of the Joint Text Draft uses the term "tested in an ABM mode," in defining ABM components, and Article VI includes certain obligations concerning such testing. We believe that the sides should have a common understanding of this phrase. First, we would note that the testing provisions of the BM Treaty are intended to apply to testing which occurs after the date of signature of the Treaty, and not to any testing which may have occurred in the past. Next, we would amplify the remarks we have made on this subject during the previous Helsinki phase by setting forth the objectives which govern the U.S. view on the subject, namely, while prohibiting testing on non-ABM components for ABM purposes: not to prevent testing of ABM components, and not to prevent testing of non-ABM components for non-ABM purposes. To clarify our interpretation of "tested in an ABM mode," we note that we would consider a launcher, missile or radar to be "tested in an ABM mode" if, for example, any of the following events occur: (1) a launcher is used to launch an ABM interceptor missile, (2) an interceptor missile is flight tested against a target vehicle which has a flight trajectory with characteristics of a strategic ballistic missile flight trajectory, or is flight tested in conjunction with the test of an ABM interceptor missile or an ABM radar at the same test range, or is flight tested to an altitude inconsistent with interception of targets against which air defenses are deployed, (3) a radar makes measurements on a cooperative target vehicle of the kind referred to in item (2) above during the reentry portion of its trajectory or makes measurements in conjunction with the test of an ABM interceptor missile or an ABM radar at the same test range. Radars used for purposes such as range safety or instrumentation would be exempt from application of these criteria.

C. No-Transfer Article of ABM Treaty

On April 18, 1972, the U.S. Delegation made the following statement:

In regard to this Article [X], I have a brief and I believe self-explanatory statement to make. The U.S. side wishes to make clear that the provisions of this Article do not set a precedent for whatever provision may be considered for a Treaty on Limiting Strategic Offensive Arms. The question of transfer of strategic offensive arms is a far more complex issue, which may require a different solution.

D. No Increase in Defense of Early Warning Radars

On July 28, 1970, the U.S. Delegation made the following statement:

Since Hen House radars [Soviet ballistic missile early warning radars] can detect and track ballistic missile warheads at great distances, they have a significant ABM potential. Accordingly, the U.S. would regard any increase in the defenses of such radars by surface-to-air missiles as inconsistent with any agreement.

PROTOCOL TO THE TREATY BETWEEN THE UNITED STATES OF AMERICA AND THE UNION OF SOVIET SOCIALIST REPUBLICS ON THE LIMITATIONS OF ANTI-BALLISTIC MISSILES

Signed at Moscow July 3, 1974
Ratification advised by U.S. Senate November 10, 1975
Ratified by U.S. President March 19, 1976
Instruments of ratification exchanged May 24, 1976
Proclaimed by U.S. President July 6, 1976
Entered into force May 24, 1976

The United States of America and the Union of Soviet Socialist Republics, hereinafter referred to as the Parties,

Proceeding from the Basic Principles of Relations between the United States of America and the Union of Soviet Socialist Republics signed on May 29, 1972,

Desiring to further the objectives of the Treaty between the United States of America and the Union of Soviet Socialist Republics on the Limitation of Anti-Ballistic Missile Systems signed on May 26, 1972, hereinafter referred to as the Treaty,

Reaffirming their conviction that the adoption of further measures for the limitation of strategic arms would contribute to strengthening international peace and security,

Proceeding from the premise that further limitation of anti-ballistic missile systems will create more favorable conditions for the completion of work on a permanent agreement on more complete measures for the limitation of strategic offensive arms,

Have agreed as follows:

Article I

1. Each Party shall be limited at any one time to a single area out of the two provided in Article III of the Treaty for deployment of anti-ballistic missile (ABM) systems or their components and accordingly shall not exercise its right to deploy an ABM system or its components in the second of the two ABM system deployment areas permitted by Article III of the Treaty, except as an exchange of one permitted area for the other in accordance with Article II of this Protocol.

2. Accordingly, except as permitted by Article II of this Protocol: the United States of America shall not deploy an ABM system or its components in the area centered on its capital, as permitted by Article III(a) of the Treaty, and the Soviet Union shall not deploy an ABM system or its components in the deployment area of intercontinental ballistic missile (ICBM) silo launchers as permitted by Article III(b) of the Treaty.

Article II

1. Each Party shall have the right to dismantle or destroy its ABM system and components thereof in the area where they are presently deployed and to deploy an ABM system or its components in the alternative area permitted by Article III of the treaty, provided that prior to initiation of construction, notification is given in accord with the procedure agreed to in the Standing Consultative Commission, during the year beginning October 3, 1977 and ending October 2, 1978, or during any year which commences at five year intervals thereafter, those being the years for periodic review of the Treaty, as provided in Article XIV of the Treaty. This right may be exercised only once.

2. Accordingly, in the event of such notice, the United States would have the right to dismantle or destroy the ABM system and its components in the deployment area of ICBM silo launchers and to deploy an ABM system or its components in an area centered on its capital, as permitted by Article III(a) of the Treaty, and the Soviet Union would have the right to dismantle or destroy the ABM system and its components in the area centered on its capital and to deploy an ABM system or its components in an area containing ICBM silo launchers, as permitted by Article III(b) of the Treaty.

3. Dismantling or destruction and deployment of ABM systems or their components and the notification thereof shall be carried out in accordance with Article VIII of the ABM Treaty and procedures agreed to in the Standing Consultative Commission.

Article III

The rights and obligations established by the Treaty remain in force and shall be complied with by the Parties except to the extent modified by this Protocol. In particular, the deployment of an ABM system or its components within the area selected shall remain limited by the levels and other requirements established by the Treaty.

Article IV
This Protocol shall be subject to ratification in accordance with the constitutional procedures of each Party. It shall enter into force on the day of the exchange of instruments of ratification and shall thereafter be considered an integral part of the Treaty.

DONE at Moscow on July 3, 1974, in duplicate, in the English and Russian languages, both texts being equally authentic.

For the United States of America:
RICHARD NIXON
President of the United States of America
For the Union of Soviet Socialist Republics:
L. I. BREZHNEV
General Secretary of the Central Committee of the CPSU

Appendix C

Glossary of Terms & Abbreviations

ABM	anti-ballistic missile designed to intercept and destroy enemy missiles and warheads
Active sensor	both a detector and a source of illumination
Acquisition	detection of a potential target by the sensors of a weapons system
AOA	airborne optical adjunct, sensors designed to detect, track, and discriminate an incoming warhead
Architecture	a physical structure of a system
ASAT	antisatellite weapon which destroys enemy military satellites
Astrodome defense	the defense of a large geographical area
ATP	acquisition, tracking, and pointing
ATSU	accelerator test stand upgrade
Battle management	the hardware and software controlling the operation of a BMD system
BMD	ballistic missile defense, designed to protect territory from attacking ballistic missiles
BM/C3	battle management/command, control and communications
Boost phase	initial flight of a missile during which the warheads are lifted by large "boost" rockets into space
Booster	rocket that lifts the warhead into a ballistic trajectory
Break-out	a technological surprise resulting in immediate abrogation of a treaty in order to rapidly build new weapon system
BSTS	boost surveillance and tracking system
Bus vehicle	it carries the multiple warheads and has maneuvering capability to place each warhead on its final trajectory to a target
Chemical laser	chemical action produces the pulses of coherent light
Countermeasures	offensive measures to overcome a BMD system

DARPA	Defense Advanced Research Projects Agency
Decoy	dummy warheads that are released from missiles along with real warhead
Directed-energy weapons	particle or laser beams that would focus intense energy on incoming enemy missiles and warheads from long distances at nearly the speed of light
Discrimination	a defensive system to distinguish between decoys and an enemy's threatening booster rocket, post-boost vehicle, or RV
DoD	Department of Defense
DoE	Department of Energy
DEW	directed energy weapons
ENDO-NNK	endoatmospheric non-nuclear kill
ERIS	exoatmospheric reentry vehicle interceptor subsystem
Excimer laser	a chemical laser; excimer is short for "excited dimer"; a dimer is a pair of linked atoms, when the bonds linking the atoms are broken, light is emitted
Exoatmospheric	activities that take place outside the earth's atmosphere, generally above 100 kilometers
EXO-NNK	exoatmospheric non-nuclear kill
Fast-burn booster	a ballistic missile that can lift its warheads faster than current vehicles, which complicates a boost-phase defense
Free-electron laser	electrons converted to coherent light
FEL	free electron laser
Hardening	making a potential target more difficult to destroy
HEDI	high endoatmospheric defense interceptor
HOE	homing overlay experiment
ICBM	intercontinental ballistic missile
Infrared sensor	detects infrared radiation from a missile or reentry vehicle
Interceptors	missiles that seek and destroy boosters or incoming enemy warheads
IR	infrared
Keep-out zone	establishing a zone around a space station that is off-limits to enemy satellites in peacetime
KEW	kinetic energy weapons
Kill assessment	detection and assimilation of information about an object under attack

Kill vehicles	rockets or projectiles that destroy enemy missiles by means of a high-speed impact
Kinetic energy	energy of momentum, used in such weapons as a rock, a bullet, and electromagnetic railgun
LAMP	large advanced mirror program
Lasant	material that can be stimulated to produce laser light
Laser	emits a narrow, highly concentrated beam of light to burn a hole through enemy missiles or warheads
Layer defenses	use of several layers of BMD at different phases of the missile trajectory; e.g., boost, post-boost, terminal phases
LODE	large optics demonstration experiment
LWIR	long wavelength infrared
MIRACL	mid-infrared advanced chemical laser
Midcourse phase	The 20-30 minutes during which the warhead is traveling through space before it reenters the atmosphere.
Neutral-particle beam	energetic beam of neutral (no electric charge) atoms, accelerates particles at nearly the speed of light
Particle-beam weapons	a highly concentrated stream of subatomic particles accelerated to nearly the speed of light
Passive discrimination	uses a non-radiating sensor to detect target emissions
Passive sensor	detects radiation naturally emitted or reflected from a target
Penetration aids	methods to defeat defenses by camouflage, deception, decoys, and countermeasures; see Decoys
Pop-up laser	is mounted on a missile that could quickly launch it into space for firing at enemy missiles
Post-boost phase	after the missile's rockets have finished firing and warheads are launched; see "Bus" and "Decoys"
Railgun	high-speed electromagnetic launcher that propels a projectile down a pair of rails with great acceleration
RV	reentry vehicle, a small container containing nuclear warheads released during the post-boost phase
SATKA	surveillance, acquisition, tracking, and kill assessment
Salvaged-fused	a warhead set to detonate when attacked
SBKKV	space-based kinetic kill vehicle
SBPB	space-based particle beam
SDI	Strategic Defense Initiative

SDIO	Strategic Defense Initiative Organization
Sensors	radar surveillance devices that "see" by detecting radio waves reflected off objects; heat sensors "feel" heat released by an object
Shoot-back	technique of defending a space station by shooting at an attacker
Software	the computer programs for instructing SDI operations
Space mines	devices that can track and follow a target in orbit that can explode on command to destroy the target
SSTS	space surveillance and tracking system
Terminal phase	final phase of an RV flight, lasting a minute or less, in which the RV reenters the atmosphere and detonates on a target
TIR	terminal imaging radar